MW00567961

2364B:
What's New in Microsoft® Visual Studio® 2005 for Existing Visual Studio .NET Developers

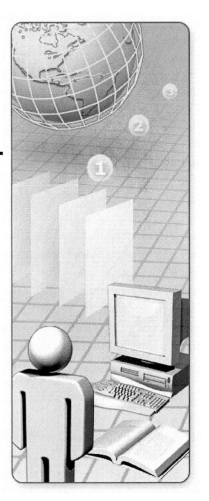

Information in this document, including URL and other Internet Web site references, is subject to change without notice. Unless otherwise noted, the example companies, organizations, products, domain names, e-mail addresses, logos, people, places, and events depicted herein are fictitious, and no association with any real company, organization, product, domain name, e-mail address, logo, person, place or event is intended or should be inferred. Complying with all applicable copyright laws is the responsibility of the user. Without limiting the rights under copyright, no part of this document may be reproduced, stored in or introduced into a retrieval system, or transmitted in any form or by any means (electronic, mechanical, photocopying, recording, or otherwise), or for any purpose, without the express written permission of Microsoft Corporation.

The names of manufacturers, products, or URLs are provided for informational purposes only and Microsoft makes no representations and warranties, either expressed, implied, or statutory, regarding these manufacturers or the use of the products with any Microsoft technologies. The inclusion of a manufacturer or product does not imply endorsement of Microsoft of the manufacturer or product. Links are provided to third party sites. Such sites are not under the control of Microsoft and Microsoft is not responsible for the contents of any linked site or any link contained in a linked site, or any changes or updates to such sites. Microsoft is not responsible for webcasting or any other form of transmission received from any linked site. Microsoft is providing these links to you only as a convenience, and the inclusion of any link does not imply endorsement of Microsoft of the site or the products contained therein.

Microsoft may have patents, patent applications, trademarks, copyrights, or other intellectual property rights covering subject matter in this document. Except as expressly provided in any written license agreement from Microsoft, the furnishing of this document does not give you any license to these patents, trademarks, copyrights, or other intellectual property.

© 2005 Microsoft Corporation. All rights reserved.

Microsoft, ActiveX, IntelliSense, MSDN, MS-DOS, PowerPoint, Visual Basic, Visual C#, Visual SourceSafe, Visual Studio, Visual Web Developer, Windows, Windows Media, Windows NT, and Windows Server are either registered trademarks or trademarks of Microsoft Corporation in the United States and/or other countries.

All other trademarks are property of their respective owners.

1 2 3 4 5 6 7 8 9   QWE   9 8 7 6 5

Clinic Number: 2364B
Part Number: X11-34317
Released: 07/2005

END-USER LICENSE AGREEMENT FOR OFFICIAL MICROSOFT LEARNING PRODUCTS – STUDENT EDITION

PLEASE READ THIS END-USER LICENSE AGREEMENT ("EULA") CAREFULLY. BY USING THE MATERIALS AND/OR USING OR INSTALLING THE SOFTWARE THAT ACCOMPANIES THIS EULA (COLLECTIVELY, THE "LICENSED CONTENT"), YOU AGREE TO THE TERMS OF THIS EULA. IF YOU DO NOT AGREE, DO NOT USE THE LICENSED CONTENT.

1.   **GENERAL.** This EULA is a legal agreement between you (either an individual or a single entity) and Microsoft Corporation ("Microsoft"). This EULA governs the Licensed Content, which includes computer software (including online and electronic documentation), training materials, and any other associated media and printed materials. This EULA applies to updates, supplements, add-on components, and Internet-based services components of the Licensed Content that Microsoft may provide or make available to you unless Microsoft provides other terms with the update, supplement, add-on component, or Internet-based services component. Microsoft reserves the right to discontinue any Internet-based services provided to you or made available to you through the use of the Licensed Content. This EULA also governs any product support services relating to the Licensed Content except as may be included in another agreement between you and Microsoft. An amendment or addendum to this EULA may accompany the Licensed Content.

2.   **GENERAL GRANT OF LICENSE.** Microsoft grants you the following rights, conditioned on your compliance with all the terms and conditions of this EULA. Microsoft grants you a limited, non-exclusive, royalty-free license to install and use the Licensed Content solely in conjunction with your participation as a student in an Authorized Training Session (as defined below). You may install and use one copy of the software on a single computer, device, workstation, terminal, or other digital electronic or analog device ("Device"). You may make a second copy of the software and install it on a portable Device for the exclusive use of the person who is the primary user of the first copy of the software. A license for the software may not be shared for use by multiple end users. An "Authorized Training Session" means a training session conducted at a Microsoft Certified Technical Education Center, an IT Academy, via a Microsoft Certified Partner, or such other entity as Microsoft may designate from time to time in writing, by a Microsoft Certified Trainer (for more information on these entities, please visit www.microsoft.com). WITHOUT LIMITING THE FOREGOING, COPYING OR REPRODUCTION OF THE LICENSED CONTENT TO ANY SERVER OR LOCATION FOR FURTHER REPRODUCTION OR REDISTRIBUTION IS EXPRESSLY PROHIBITED.

3.   **DESCRIPTION OF OTHER RIGHTS AND LICENSE LIMITATIONS**

   3.1   *Use of Documentation and Printed Training Materials.*

      3.1.1   The documents and related graphics included in the Licensed Content may include technical inaccuracies or typographical errors. Changes are periodically made to the content. Microsoft may make improvements and/or changes in any of the components of the Licensed Content at any time without notice. The names of companies, products, people, characters and/or data mentioned in the Licensed Content may be fictitious and are in no way intended to represent any real individual, company, product or event, unless otherwise noted.

      3.1.2   Microsoft grants you the right to reproduce portions of documents (such as student workbooks, white papers, press releases, datasheets and FAQs) (the "Documents") provided with the Licensed Content. You may not print any book (either electronic or print version) in its entirety. If you choose to reproduce Documents, you agree that: (a) use of such printed Documents will be solely in conjunction with your personal training use; (b) the Documents will not republished or posted on any network computer or broadcast in any media; (c) any reproduction will include either the Document's original copyright notice or a copyright notice to Microsoft's benefit substantially in the format provided below; and (d) to comply with all terms and conditions of this EULA. In addition, no modifications may made to any Document.

   Form of Notice:

   Copyright undefined.

   © 2005. Reprinted with permission by Microsoft Corporation. All rights reserved.

   Microsoft and Windows are either registered trademarks or trademarks of Microsoft Corporation in the US and/or other countries. Other product and company names mentioned herein may be the trademarks of their respective owners.

   3.2   *Use of Media Elements.* The Licensed Content may include certain photographs, clip art, animations, sounds, music, and video clips (together "Media Elements"). You may not modify these Media Elements.

   3.3   *Use of Sample Code.* In the event that the Licensed Content include sample source code ("Sample Code"), Microsoft grants you a limited, non-exclusive, royalty-free license to use, copy and modify the Sample Code; if you elect to exercise the foregoing rights, you agree to comply with all other terms and conditions of this EULA, including without limitation Sections 3.4, 3.5, and 6.

   3.4   *Permitted Modifications.* In the event that you exercise any rights provided under this EULA to create modifications of the Licensed Content, you agree that any such modifications: (a) will not be used for providing training where a fee is charged in public or private classes; (b) indemnify, hold harmless, and defend Microsoft from and against any claims or lawsuits, including attorneys' fees, which arise from or result from your use of any modified version of the Licensed Content; and (c) not to transfer or assign any rights to any modified version of the Licensed Content to any third party without the express written permission of Microsoft.

3.5   *Reproduction/Redistribution Licensed Content.* Except as expressly provided in this EULA, you may not reproduce or distribute the Licensed Content or any portion thereof (including any permitted modifications) to any third parties without the express written permission of Microsoft.

4.   **RESERVATION OF RIGHTS AND OWNERSHIP.** Microsoft reserves all rights not expressly granted to you in this EULA. The Licensed Content is protected by copyright and other intellectual property laws and treaties. Microsoft or its suppliers own the title, copyright, and other intellectual property rights in the Licensed Content. You may not remove or obscure any copyright, trademark or patent notices that appear on the Licensed Content, or any components thereof, as delivered to you. **The Licensed Content is licensed, not sold.**

5.   **LIMITATIONS ON REVERSE ENGINEERING, DECOMPILATION, AND DISASSEMBLY.** You may not reverse engineer, decompile, or disassemble the Software or Media Elements, except and only to the extent that such activity is expressly permitted by applicable law notwithstanding this limitation.

6.   **LIMITATIONS ON SALE, RENTAL, ETC. AND CERTAIN ASSIGNMENTS.** You may not provide commercial hosting services with, sell, rent, lease, lend, sublicense, or assign copies of the Licensed Content, or any portion thereof (including any permitted modifications thereof) on a stand-alone basis or as part of any collection, product or service.

7.   **CONSENT TO USE OF DATA.** You agree that Microsoft and its affiliates may collect and use technical information gathered as part of the product support services provided to you, if any, related to the Licensed Content. Microsoft may use this information solely to improve our products or to provide customized services or technologies to you and will not disclose this information in a form that personally identifies you.

8.   **LINKS TO THIRD PARTY SITES.** You may link to third party sites through the use of the Licensed Content. The third party sites are not under the control of Microsoft, and Microsoft is not responsible for the contents of any third party sites, any links contained in third party sites, or any changes or updates to third party sites. Microsoft is not responsible for webcasting or any other form of transmission received from any third party sites. Microsoft is providing these links to third party sites to you only as a convenience, and the inclusion of any link does not imply an endorsement by Microsoft of the third party site.

9.   **ADDITIONAL LICENSED CONTENT/SERVICES.** This EULA applies to updates, supplements, add-on components, or Internet-based services components, of the Licensed Content that Microsoft may provide to you or make available to you after the date you obtain your initial copy of the Licensed Content, unless we provide other terms along with the update, supplement, add-on component, or Internet-based services component. Microsoft reserves the right to discontinue any Internet-based services provided to you or made available to you through the use of the Licensed Content.

10.   **U.S. GOVERNMENT LICENSE RIGHTS.** All software provided to the U.S. Government pursuant to solicitations issued on or after December 1, 1995 is provided with the commercial license rights and restrictions described elsewhere herein. All software provided to the U.S. Government pursuant to solicitations issued prior to December 1, 1995 is provided with "Restricted Rights" as provided for in FAR, 48 CFR 52.227-14 (JUNE 1987) or DFAR, 48 CFR 252.227-7013 (OCT 1988), as applicable.

11.   **EXPORT RESTRICTIONS.** You acknowledge that the Licensed Content is subject to U.S. export jurisdiction. You agree to comply with all applicable international and national laws that apply to the Licensed Content, including the U.S. Export Administration Regulations, as well as end-user, end-use, and destination restrictions issued by U.S. and other governments. For additional information see <http://www.microsoft.com/exporting/>.

12.   **TRANSFER.** The initial user of the Licensed Content may make a one-time permanent transfer of this EULA and Licensed Content to another end user, provided the initial user retains no copies of the Licensed Content. The transfer may not be an indirect transfer, such as a consignment. Prior to the transfer, the end user receiving the Licensed Content must agree to all the EULA terms.

13.   **"NOT FOR RESALE" LICENSED CONTENT.** Licensed Content identified as "Not For Resale" or "NFR," may not be sold or otherwise transferred for value, or used for any purpose other than demonstration, test or evaluation.

14.   **TERMINATION.** Without prejudice to any other rights, Microsoft may terminate this EULA if you fail to comply with the terms and conditions of this EULA. In such event, you must destroy all copies of the Licensed Content and all of its component parts.

15.   **DISCLAIMER OF WARRANTIES. TO THE MAXIMUM EXTENT PERMITTED BY APPLICABLE LAW, MICROSOFT AND ITS SUPPLIERS PROVIDE THE LICENSED CONTENT AND SUPPORT SERVICES (IF ANY)** *AS IS AND WITH ALL FAULTS,* **AND MICROSOFT AND ITS SUPPLIERS HEREBY DISCLAIM ALL OTHER WARRANTIES AND CONDITIONS, WHETHER EXPRESS, IMPLIED OR STATUTORY, INCLUDING, BUT NOT LIMITED TO, ANY (IF ANY) IMPLIED WARRANTIES, DUTIES OR CONDITIONS OF MERCHANTABILITY, OF FITNESS FOR A PARTICULAR PURPOSE, OF RELIABILITY OR AVAILABILITY, OF ACCURACY OR COMPLETENESS OF RESPONSES, OF RESULTS, OF WORKMANLIKE EFFORT, OF LACK OF VIRUSES, AND OF LACK OF NEGLIGENCE, ALL WITH REGARD TO THE LICENSED CONTENT, AND THE PROVISION OF OR FAILURE TO PROVIDE SUPPORT OR OTHER SERVICES, INFORMATION, SOFTWARE, AND RELATED CONTENT THROUGH THE LICENSED CONTENT, OR OTHERWISE ARISING OUT OF THE USE OF THE LICENSED CONTENT. ALSO, THERE IS NO WARRANTY OR CONDITION OF TITLE, QUIET ENJOYMENT, QUIET POSSESSION, CORRESPONDENCE TO DESCRIPTION OR NON-INFRINGEMENT WITH REGARD TO THE LICENSED CONTENT. THE ENTIRE RISK AS TO THE QUALITY, OR ARISING OUT OF THE USE OR PERFORMANCE OF THE LICENSED CONTENT, AND ANY SUPPORT SERVICES, REMAINS WITH YOU.**

16.   **EXCLUSION OF INCIDENTAL, CONSEQUENTIAL AND CERTAIN OTHER DAMAGES. TO THE MAXIMUM EXTENT PERMITTED BY APPLICABLE LAW, IN NO EVENT SHALL MICROSOFT OR ITS SUPPLIERS BE LIABLE FOR ANY SPECIAL, INCIDENTAL, PUNITIVE, INDIRECT, OR CONSEQUENTIAL DAMAGES WHATSOEVER (INCLUDING, BUT NOT**

LIMITED TO, DAMAGES FOR LOSS OF PROFITS OR CONFIDENTIAL OR OTHER INFORMATION, FOR BUSINESS INTERRUPTION, FOR PERSONAL INJURY, FOR LOSS OF PRIVACY, FOR FAILURE TO MEET ANY DUTY INCLUDING OF GOOD FAITH OR OF REASONABLE CARE, FOR NEGLIGENCE, AND FOR ANY OTHER PECUNIARY OR OTHER LOSS WHATSOEVER) ARISING OUT OF OR IN ANY WAY RELATED TO THE USE OF OR INABILITY TO USE THE LICENSED CONTENT, THE PROVISION OF OR FAILURE TO PROVIDE SUPPORT OR OTHER SERVICES, INFORMATION, SOFTWARE, AND RELATED CONTENT THROUGH THE LICENSED CONTENT, OR OTHERWISE ARISING OUT OF THE USE OF THE LICENSED CONTENT, OR OTHERWISE UNDER OR IN CONNECTION WITH ANY PROVISION OF THIS EULA, EVEN IN THE EVENT OF THE FAULT, TORT (INCLUDING NEGLIGENCE), MISREPRESENTATION, STRICT LIABILITY, BREACH OF CONTRACT OR BREACH OF WARRANTY OF MICROSOFT OR ANY SUPPLIER, AND EVEN IF MICROSOFT OR ANY SUPPLIER HAS BEEN ADVISED OF THE POSSIBILITY OF SUCH DAMAGES. BECAUSE SOME STATES/JURISDICTIONS DO NOT ALLOW THE EXCLUSION OR LIMITATION OF LIABILITY FOR CONSEQUENTIAL OR INCIDENTAL DAMAGES, THE ABOVE LIMITATION MAY NOT APPLY TO YOU.

17. **LIMITATION OF LIABILITY AND REMEDIES.** NOTWITHSTANDING ANY DAMAGES THAT YOU MIGHT INCUR FOR ANY REASON WHATSOEVER (INCLUDING, WITHOUT LIMITATION, ALL DAMAGES REFERENCED HEREIN AND ALL DIRECT OR GENERAL DAMAGES IN CONTRACT OR ANYTHING ELSE), THE ENTIRE LIABILITY OF MICROSOFT AND ANY OF ITS SUPPLIERS UNDER ANY PROVISION OF THIS EULA AND YOUR EXCLUSIVE REMEDY HEREUNDER SHALL BE LIMITED TO THE GREATER OF THE ACTUAL DAMAGES YOU INCUR IN REASONABLE RELIANCE ON THE LICENSED CONTENT UP TO THE AMOUNT ACTUALLY PAID BY YOU FOR THE LICENSED CONTENT OR US$5.00. THE FOREGOING LIMITATIONS, EXCLUSIONS AND DISCLAIMERS SHALL APPLY TO THE MAXIMUM EXTENT PERMITTED BY APPLICABLE LAW, EVEN IF ANY REMEDY FAILS ITS ESSENTIAL PURPOSE.

18. **APPLICABLE LAW.** If you acquired this Licensed Content in the United States, this EULA is governed by the laws of the State of Washington. If you acquired this Licensed Content in Canada, unless expressly prohibited by local law, this EULA is governed by the laws in force in the Province of Ontario, Canada; and, in respect of any dispute which may arise hereunder, you consent to the jurisdiction of the federal and provincial courts sitting in Toronto, Ontario. If you acquired this Licensed Content in the European Union, Iceland, Norway, or Switzerland, then local law applies. If you acquired this Licensed Content in any other country, then local law may apply.

19. **ENTIRE AGREEMENT; SEVERABILITY.** This EULA (including any addendum or amendment to this EULA which is included with the Licensed Content) are the entire agreement between you and Microsoft relating to the Licensed Content and the support services (if any) and they supersede all prior or contemporaneous oral or written communications, proposals and representations with respect to the Licensed Content or any other subject matter covered by this EULA. To the extent the terms of any Microsoft policies or programs for support services conflict with the terms of this EULA, the terms of this EULA shall control. If any provision of this EULA is held to be void, invalid, unenforceable or illegal, the other provisions shall continue in full force and effect.

Should you have any questions concerning this EULA, or if you desire to contact Microsoft for any reason, please use the address information enclosed in this Licensed Content to contact the Microsoft subsidiary serving your country or visit Microsoft on the World Wide Web at http://www.microsoft.com.

Si vous avez acquis votre Contenu Sous Licence Microsoft au CANADA :

DÉNI DE GARANTIES. Dans la mesure maximale permise par les lois applicables, le Contenu Sous Licence et les services de soutien technique (le cas échéant) sont fournis *TELS QUELS ET AVEC TOUS LES DÉFAUTS* par Microsoft et ses fournisseurs, lesquels par les présentes dénient toutes autres garanties et conditions expresses, implicites ou en vertu de la loi, notamment, mais sans limitation, (le cas échéant) les garanties, devoirs ou conditions implicites de qualité marchande, d'adaptation à une fin usage particulière, de fiabilité ou de disponibilité, d'exactitude ou d'exhaustivité des réponses, des résultats, des efforts déployés selon les règles de l'art, d'absence de virus et d'absence de négligence, le tout à l'égard du Contenu Sous Licence et de la prestation des services de soutien technique ou de l'omission de la 'une telle prestation des services de soutien technique ou à l'égard de la fourniture ou de l'omission de la fourniture de tous autres services, renseignements, Contenus Sous Licence, et contenu qui s'y rapporte grâce au Contenu Sous Licence ou provenant autrement de l'utilisation du Contenu Sous Licence. PAR AILLEURS, IL N'Y A AUCUNE GARANTIE OU CONDITION QUANT AU TITRE DE PROPRIÉTÉ, À LA JOUISSANCE OU LA POSSESSION PAISIBLE, À LA CONCORDANCE À UNE DESCRIPTION NI QUANT À UNE ABSENCE DE CONTREFAÇON CONCERNANT LE CONTENU SOUS LICENCE.

EXCLUSION DES DOMMAGES ACCESSOIRES, INDIRECTS ET DE CERTAINS AUTRES DOMMAGES. DANS LA MESURE MAXIMALE PERMISE PAR LES LOIS APPLICABLES, EN AUCUN CAS MICROSOFT OU SES FOURNISSEURS NE SERONT RESPONSABLES DES DOMMAGES SPÉCIAUX, CONSÉCUTIFS, ACCESSOIRES OU INDIRECTS DE QUELQUE NATURE QUE CE SOIT (NOTAMMENT, LES DOMMAGES À L'ÉGARD DU MANQUE À GAGNER OU DE LA DIVULGATION DE RENSEIGNEMENTS CONFIDENTIELS OU AUTRES, DE LA PERTE D'EXPLOITATION, DE BLESSURES CORPORELLES, DE LA VIOLATION DE LA VIE PRIVÉE, DE L'OMISSION DE REMPLIR TOUT DEVOIR, Y COMPRIS D'AGIR DE BONNE FOI OU D'EXERCER UN SOIN RAISONNABLE, DE LA NÉGLIGENCE ET DE TOUTE AUTRE PERTE PÉCUNIAIRE OU AUTRE PERTE

DE QUELQUE NATURE QUE CE SOIT) SE RAPPORTANT DE QUELQUE MANIÈRE QUE CE SOIT À L'UTILISATION DU CONTENU SOUS LICENCE OU À L'INCAPACITÉ DE S'EN SERVIR, À LA PRESTATION OU À L'OMISSION DE LA 'UNE TELLE PRESTATION DE SERVICES DE SOUTIEN TECHNIQUE OU À LA FOURNITURE OU À L'OMISSION DE LA FOURNITURE DE TOUS AUTRES SERVICES, RENSEIGNEMENTS, CONTENUS SOUS LICENCE, ET CONTENU QUI S'Y RAPPORTE GRÂCE AU CONTENU SOUS LICENCE OU PROVENANT AUTREMENT DE L'UTILISATION DU CONTENU SOUS LICENCE OU AUTREMENT AUX TERMES DE TOUTE DISPOSITION DE LA U PRÉSENTE CONVENTION EULA OU RELATIVEMENT À UNE TELLE DISPOSITION, MÊME EN CAS DE FAUTE, DE DÉLIT CIVIL (Y COMPRIS LA NÉGLIGENCE), DE RESPONSABILITÉ STRICTE, DE VIOLATION DE CONTRAT OU DE VIOLATION DE GARANTIE DE MICROSOFT OU DE TOUT FOURNISSEUR ET MÊME SI MICROSOFT OU TOUT FOURNISSEUR A ÉTÉ AVISÉ DE LA POSSIBILITÉ DE TELS DOMMAGES.

LIMITATION DE RESPONSABILITÉ ET RECOURS. MALGRÉ LES DOMMAGES QUE VOUS PUISSIEZ SUBIR POUR QUELQUE MOTIF QUE CE SOIT (NOTAMMENT, MAIS SANS LIMITATION, TOUS LES DOMMAGES SUSMENTIONNÉS ET TOUS LES DOMMAGES DIRECTS OU GÉNÉRAUX OU AUTRES), LA SEULE RESPONSABILITÉ 'OBLIGATION INTÉGRALE DE MICROSOFT ET DE L'UN OU L'AUTRE DE SES FOURNISSEURS AUX TERMES DE TOUTE DISPOSITION DEU LA PRÉSENTE CONVENTION EULA ET VOTRE RECOURS EXCLUSIF À L'ÉGARD DE TOUT CE QUI PRÉCÈDE SE LIMITE AU PLUS ÉLEVÉ ENTRE LES MONTANTS SUIVANTS : LE MONTANT QUE VOUS AVEZ RÉELLEMENT PAYÉ POUR LE CONTENU SOUS LICENCE OU 5,00 $US. LES LIMITES, EXCLUSIONS ET DÉNIS QUI PRÉCÈDENT (Y COMPRIS LES CLAUSES CI-DESSUS), S'APPLIQUENT DANS LA MESURE MAXIMALE PERMISE PAR LES LOIS APPLICABLES, MÊME SI TOUT RECOURS N'ATTEINT PAS SON BUT ESSENTIEL.

À moins que cela ne soit prohibé par le droit local applicable, la présente Convention est régie par les lois de la province d'Ontario, Canada. Vous consentez Chacune des parties à la présente reconnaît irrévocablement à la compétence des tribunaux fédéraux et provinciaux siégeant à Toronto, dans de la province d'Ontario et consent à instituer tout litige qui pourrait découler de la présente auprès des tribunaux situés dans le district judiciaire de York, province d'Ontario.

Au cas où vous auriez des questions concernant cette licence ou que vous désiriez vous mettre en rapport avec Microsoft pour quelque raison que ce soit, veuillez utiliser l'information contenue dans le Contenu Sous Licence pour contacter la filiale de succursale Microsoft desservant votre pays, dont l'adresse est fournie dans ce produit, ou visitez écrivez à : Microsoft sur le World Wide Web à http://www.microsoft.com

Contents

About This Workshop

This section provides you with a brief description of the workshop, audience, suggested prerequisites, and workshop objectives.

Description

This workshop provides the students with hands-on experience with the features and functionality of Microsoft® Visual Studio® 2005 that are either new or significantly enhanced from Visual Studio .NET 2003.

Audience

This workshop is intended for experienced, professional software developers, including those employed by independent software vendors or those who work on corporate enterprise development teams, who are already skilled at using Visual Studio .NET or Visual Studio .NET 2003 to build software. Students in this workshop should have a 200 or 300 skill level as Visual Studio .NET developers. They should also have at least one year of development experience using Visual Studio .NET and/or Visual Studio .NET 2003 with the Microsoft Visual Basic® .NET or Microsoft Visual C#® programming languages. The workshop format is intended for students who learn best by doing hands-on work.

Student prerequisites

This workshop requires that students meet the following prerequisites:

- At least one year of experience using Visual Studio .NET or Visual Studio .NET 2003 as a full-time developer
- Experience developing one or more of the following:
  - Web applications
  - Microsoft Windows® Forms applications
  - Server components

Workshop objectives

After completing this workshop, the student will be able to:

- Develop software more efficiently.
- Write applications that use Visual Basic and Visual C# programming language enhancements.
- Build managed code to run inside Microsoft SQL Server™ 2005.
- Write data access code using the improved functionality in ADO.NET.
- Build Windows Forms applications using the new controls and new functionality in the Visual Studio .NET Integrated Development Environment (IDE) designers.
- Deploy rich client applications by using the new ClickOnce application deployment functionality.
- Build ASP.NET Web applications using the new controls and new functionality in the Visual Studio .NET IDE designers.

Preparation Tasks

To prepare for this workshop, you must:

- Complete the Workshop Preparation Checklist that is included with the trainer materials.

- Perform all workshop labs.

- Review the Technical Specification documents and e-mail messages in the Lab Toolkit.

- For each unit, familiarize yourself with the resources on the **Scenario** tab and the **Resources** tab in the Lab Toolkit.

Workshop Design

The workshop uses a scenario based on building of a three-tier enterprise application for the fictitious enterprise Northwind Traders. The units are structured so that work on the database is performed first, and then data access components are constructed, followed by construction of Web, Windows Forms, and mobile presentation tier applications.

Many of the units include demonstrations. Where applicable, the procedures in these demonstrations are provided in two versions: one using Visual Basic and one using Visual C#. Use the language most appropriate to the audience when performing the demonstrations. If a module contains a demonstration or procedure that is not labeled for a particular programming language, then it is applicable to both Visual Basic and Visual C#.

The Northwind database, rather than the AdventureWorks database, is used because its simplicity allows students to concentrate on the new features in Visual Studio. Because the Northwind database is familiar to many developers experienced with earlier versions of Visual Studio and SQL Server, inform students that the new techniques they learn in this course may also be applied to their own existing database applications.

Each lab is supported by a number of Lab Toolkit resources. The most important of these is the Technical Specification, a program design document similar to a program specification that many students use when developing software at work. The student should work with this document and the lab instructions to perform the lab and should use the other toolkit resources to help with specific tasks in the lab.

Student Materials Compact Disc Contents

The Student Materials compact disc (CD) contains the following files and folders:

- *Autorun.inf.* When the CD is inserted into the CD drive, this file opens Autorun.exe.

- *Default.htm.* This file opens the Student Materials Web page. It provides you with resources pertaining to this workshop, including additional reading, review and lab answers, lab files, multimedia presentations, and workshop-related Web sites.

- *Readme.txt.* This file explains how to install the software for viewing the Student Materials CD and its contents and how to open the Student Materials Web page.

- *StartCD.exe.* When the compact disc is inserted into the CD drive, or when you double-click the **StartCD.exe** file, this file opens the CD and allows you to browse the Student Materials compact disc.

- *StartCD.ini.* This file contains instructions to launch StartCD.exe.

- *Flash.* This folder contains the installer for the Macromedia Flash 5.0 browser plug-in.

- *Fonts.* This folder contains fonts that may be required to view the Microsoft Word documents that are included with this workshop.

- *Media.* This folder contains files that are used in multimedia presentations for this workshop.

- *Mplayer.* This folder contains the setup file to install Microsoft Windows Media® Player.

- *Toolkit.* This folder contains the files for the Lab Toolkit.

- *Webfiles.* This folder contains the files that are required to view the workshop Web page. To open the Web page, open Windows Explorer, and in the root directory of the CD, double-click **StartCD.exe**.

- *Wordview.* This folder contains the Word Viewer that is used to view any Word document (.doc) files that are included on the CD.

Document Conventions

The following conventions are used in workshop materials to distinguish elements of the text.

Convention	Use
	Represents resources available by launching the Lab Toolkit shortcut on the desktop.
Bold	Represents commands, command options, and syntax that must be typed exactly as shown. It also indicates commands on menus and buttons, dialog box titles and options, and icon and menu names.
Italic	In syntax statements or descriptive text, indicates argument names or placeholders for variable information. Italic is also used for introducing new terms, for book titles, and for emphasis in the text.
Title Capitals	Indicate domain names, user names, computer names, directory names, and folder and file names, except when specifically referring to case-sensitive names. Unless otherwise indicated, you can use lowercase letters when you type a directory name or file name in a dialog box or at a command prompt.
ALL CAPITALS	Indicate the names of keys, key sequences, and key combinations—for example, ALT+SPACEBAR.
monospace	Represents code samples or examples of screen text.
[ ]	In syntax statements, enclose optional items. For example, [*filename*] in command syntax indicates that you can choose to type a file name with the command. Type only the information within the brackets, not the brackets themselves.
{ }	In syntax statements, enclose required items. Type only the information within the braces, not the braces themselves.
|	In syntax statements, separates an either/or choice.
▶	Indicates a procedure with sequential steps.
...	In syntax statements, specifies that the preceding item may be repeated.
. . .	Represents an omitted portion of a code sample.

Introduction

Contents

Information in this document, including URL and other Internet Web site references, is subject to change without notice. Unless otherwise noted, the example companies, organizations, products, domain names, e-mail addresses, logos, people, places, and events depicted herein are fictitious, and no association with any real company, organization, product, domain name, e-mail address, logo, person, place or event is intended or should be inferred. Complying with all applicable copyright laws is the responsibility of the user. Without limiting the rights under copyright, no part of this document may be reproduced, stored in or introduced into a retrieval system, or transmitted in any form or by any means (electronic, mechanical, photocopying, recording, or otherwise), or for any purpose, without the express written permission of Microsoft Corporation.

The names of manufacturers, products, or URLs are provided for informational purposes only and Microsoft makes no representations and warranties, either expressed, implied, or statutory, regarding these manufacturers or the use of the products with any Microsoft technologies. The inclusion of a manufacturer or product does not imply endorsement of Microsoft of the manufacturer or product. Links are provided to third party sites. Such sites are not under the control of Microsoft and Microsoft is not responsible for the contents of any linked site or any link contained in a linked site, or any changes or updates to such sites. Microsoft is not responsible for webcasting or any other form of transmission received from any linked site. Microsoft is providing these links to you only as a convenience, and the inclusion of any link does not imply endorsement of Microsoft of the site or the products contained therein.

Microsoft may have patents, patent applications, trademarks, copyrights, or other intellectual property rights covering subject matter in this document. Except as expressly provided in any written license agreement from Microsoft, the furnishing of this document does not give you any license to these patents, trademarks, copyrights, or other intellectual property.

© 2005 Microsoft Corporation. All rights reserved.

Microsoft, ActiveX, IntelliSense, MSDN, MS-DOS, PowerPoint, Visual Basic, Visual C#, Visual SourceSafe, Visual Studio, Visual Web Developer, Windows, Windows Media, Windows NT, and Windows Server are either registered trademarks or trademarks of Microsoft Corporation in the United States and/or other countries.

All other trademarks are property of their respective owners.

Introduction

- Name
- Company affiliation
- Title/function
- Job responsibility
- Programming and database experience
- Visual Studio .NET experience
- Expectations for the workshop

Workshop Materials

- **Name card**
- **Student workbook**
- **Student Materials compact disc**
- **Workshop evaluation**

The following materials are included with your kit:

- *Name card*. Write your name on both sides of the name card.

- *Student workbook*. The student workbook contains the material covered in class, in addition to the hands-on lab exercises.

- *Lab Toolkit*. The Lab Toolkit is an online interface that contains resources that you will use in this workshop's scenario-based labs. The toolkit video presentations, lab scenario information, and resources, such as procedures and annotated screenshots, which will help you complete the labs.

- *Student Materials compact disc*. The Student Materials compact disc contains a Web page that provides you with links to resources pertaining to this workshop, including additional readings, lab files, multimedia presentations, and workshop-related Web sites.

 Note To open the Web page, insert the Student Materials compact disc into the CD-ROM drive, and then in the root directory of the compact disc, double-click **StartCD.exe**.

- *Workshop evaluation*. Near the end of the workshop, you will have the opportunity to complete an online evaluation to provide feedback on the workshop, training facility, and instructor.

  To provide additional comments or feedback on the workshop, send e-mail to support@mscourseware.com. To inquire about the Microsoft® Certified Professional program, send e-mail to mcphelp@microsoft.com.

Prerequisites

This workshop requires that you meet the following prerequisites:

- **Experience (at least 1 year) as a full-time developer using Visual Studio .NET 2002 or Visual Studio .NET 2003**

- **Experience of working in one or more of the following fields:**
  - Web Application development
  - Windows Forms Application development
  - Server Component development
  - XML Web Services development

This workshop requires that you meet the following prerequisites:

- At least one year of experience as a full-time developer using Microsoft Visual Studio® .NET 2002 or Visual Studio .NET 2003

- Experience working in one or more of the following fields:
  - Web-based application development
  - Windows Forms application development
  - Server component development
  - XML Web Services development

Workshop Outline

- **Unit 1: Introduction to Visual Studio 2005**
- **Unit 2: Building Managed Code for SQL Server 2005**
- **Unit 3: Building Data Components in Visual Studio 2005**
- **Unit 4: Building Presentation Layer Applications with Windows Forms**
- **Unit 5: Building Presentation Layer Applications with ASP.NET 2.0**

Unit 1, "Introduction to Visual Studio 2005," introduces the major new release of Visual Studio 2005, the comprehensive development environment for building Microsoft .NET–connected applications for Microsoft Windows® and the Web. After completing this unit, you will be able to identify the major new features of Visual Studio 2005 as addressed in this workshop.

Unit 2, "Building Managed Code for SQL Server 2005," introduces the Visual Studio 2005 features that help you create the managed code that runs inside Microsoft SQL Server™ 2005. After completing this unit, you will be able to build a managed assembly that runs inside of SQL Server 2005.

Unit 3, "Building Data Components in Visual Studio 2005," introduces the new data design tools in Visual Studio 2005 and discusses the new programming features of Microsoft ADO.NET in the Microsoft .NET Framework version 2.0. After completing this unit, you will be able to use Visual Studio 2005 to create data components.

Unit 4, "Building Presentation Layer Applications with Windows Forms," introduces the new features in Windows Forms and the new deployment tools and capability available for Windows Forms applications in Visual Studio 2005. The first two labs introduce the new features for building Windows Forms applications, and in the third lab, you will create and deploy applications that auto-install on remote machines and auto-update when program updates are available. After completing this unit, you will be able to build Windows Forms applications in Visual Studio 2005 and to use "ClickOnce" to deploy Windows Forms applications.

Unit 5, "Building Presentation Layer Applications with ASP.NET 2.0," introduces the new features in ASP.NET. The three labs explore the new capabilities of ASP.NET 2.0 and the Visual Studio 2005 tools for building Web applications. After completing this unit, you will be able to build Web applications in Visual Studio 2005.

Workshop Organization

Day 1	
9:00 - 9:30	**Introductions**
9:30 - 11:30	• **Lab 1:** Programming using Productivity Enhancements and Language Improvements
11:30 - 4:00	• **Lab 2A:** Writing Managed Code for SQL Server 2005 • **Lab 2B:** Working with XML in Visual Studio 2005 and SQL Server 2005

Day 2	
9:30 - 12:00	• **Lab 3:** Accessing Data with ADO.NET
1:00 - 3:00	• **Lab 4A:** RAD Data Binding in Windows Forms
3:00 - 5:00	• **Lab 5A:** RAD Data Binding with ASP.NET 2.0

Day 3	
9:30 - 12:15	• **Lab 4B:** Data Binding to Components and Web Services • **Lab 4C:** Publishing Using ClickOnce
1:15 - 4:45	• **Lab 5B:** Programming Master Pages, Site Navigation, and Themes • **Lab 5C:** Membership and Role Management in ASP.NET 2.0

This workshop is designed to run over the course of three days. You will probably find that you do not have enough time to complete all the labs.

You will work through Units 1 through 3, but on the second day, after your instructor delivers the presentation for Unit 4, "Building Presentation Layer Application with Windows Forms," you will work through Lab 4A, "RAD Data Binding in Windows Forms." You will not work through Labs 4B or 4C at this time. Your instructor will then deliver the presentation for Unit 5, "Building Presentation Layer Applications with ASP.NET 2.0," and you will work through Lab 5A, "RAD Data Binding with ASP.NET 2.0." This completes the second day.

On the third day, you will complete the following four labs:

- Lab 4B, "Data Binding to Components and Web Services"
- Lab 4C, "Publishing Using ClickOnce"
- Lab 5B, "Programming Master Pages, Site Navigation, and Themes"
- Lab 5C, "Membership and Role Management in ASP.NET 2.0"

Setup

Setup Information	Description
Virtual Computers	London Unit 1 is the virtual computer required to perform labs in Unit 1 only. It is running Visual Studio 2005 Beta 2 and SQL Server 2005 CTP London is your primary virtual computer. It is running Visual Studio 2005 Beta 2 and SQL Server 2005 CTP *Denver* is the virtual computer running Windows XP Professional. You need this virtual computer to perform one lab in Unit 4
Course Files	Lab files are in the E:\Microsoft Learning\ 2364\Labfiles folder on London
Classroom Setup	The student computers are not networked together. You can perform all the labs using the virtual computers

Virtual Computers

The labs for this workshop are performed on virtual computers. You have access to two virtual computers:

- London is your primary virtual computer. You will perform nearly all the labs using this computer. London is running the following software:
  - Windows XP Professional
  - Visual Studio 2005 Beta 1
  - SQL Server 2005 Beta 2
- Denver is the virtual computer that you will use for one lab in Unit 4. Denver is running the following software:
  - Windows XP Professional

Workshop Files

There are files associated with the labs in this course. The lab files are located in the folder E:\Microsoft Learning\2364\Labfiles\Lab*XX*, where xx stands for the module number, on the student computers.

Classroom Setup

Each student computer in the classroom is standalone: it is not networked to any other computer in the classroom. However, the two virtual computers, London and Denver, are networked together on a private network.

Beta Software Products

* **This course uses**
    * Visual Studio 2005 Beta 2
    * SQL Server 2005 CTP

  Microsoft
  Visual Studio 2005

* **These are beta products**
    * Product features used in this course are not guaranteed to be available in the final product versions
    * This course does not describe future or anticipated features of the final products

This course describes features and functionality in the beta 1 release of Visual Studio 2005 and in the beta 2 release of SQL Server 2005. It does not describe features of the final Visual Studio 2005 product that might be added after the beta 1 release, nor does it guarantee that features described in the course will be included in the final product. When the final version of Visual Studio 2005 is available, this course will be re-tested, revised where appropriate, re-titled, and then re-released.

Because this workshop is based upon a pre-released version of Visual Studio 2005, you can expect to see in it the Integrated Development Environment (IDE) signs of a software project in process. That is, Visual Studio might crash or behave strangely. You might have to restart the IDE in order to clear an error condition.

Demonstration: Using Microsoft Virtual PC

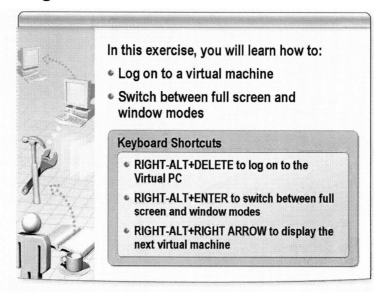

In this exercise, you will learn how to:

* Log on to a virtual machine
* Switch between full screen and window modes

Keyboard Shortcuts

* RIGHT-ALT+DELETE to log on to the Virtual PC
* RIGHT-ALT+ENTER to switch between full screen and window modes
* RIGHT-ALT+RIGHT ARROW to display the next virtual machine

In this demonstration, your instructor will help familiarize you with the Microsoft Virtual PC environment in which you will work to complete the labs in this workshop. You will learn:

- How to open Virtual PC.

- How to start Virtual PC.

- How to log on to Virtual PC.

- How to switch between full screen and window modes.

- How to tell the difference between the virtual machines that are used in the practices for this workshop.

- That the virtual machines can communicate with each other and with the host, but they cannot communicate with other computers that are outside of the virtual environment. (For example, no Internet access is available from the virtual environment.)

- How to close Virtual PC.

Keyboard Shortcuts

While working in the Virtual PC environment, you might find it helpful to use keyboard shortcuts. All Virtual PC shortcuts include a key that is referred to as the HOST key or the RIGHT-ALT key. By default, the HOST key is the ALT key on the right side of your keyboard. Some useful shortcuts include:

- ALT+DELETE to log on to the Virtual PC

- ALT+ENTER to switch between full screen mode and window modes

- ALT+RIGHT ARROW to display the next Virtual PC

For more information about Virtual PC, see Virtual PC Help.

Microsoft Learning

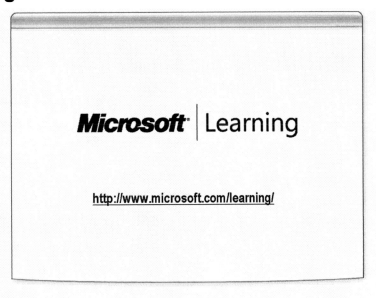

Microsoft Learning develops Official Microsoft Learning Products for computer professionals who use Microsoft products and technologies to design, develop, support, implement, or manage solutions. These learning products provide comprehensive, skills-based training in instructor-led and online formats.

Microsoft Learning Information

For more information, visit the Microsoft Learning Web site at http://www.microsoft.com/learning/.

Microsoft Learning Product Types

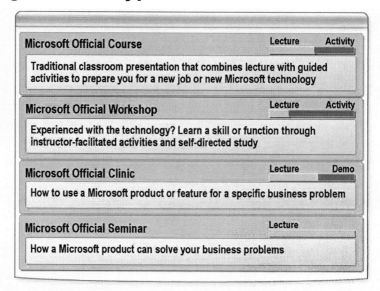

Microsoft Learning offers four types of instructor-led products. Each is specific to a particular audience type and level of experience. The different product types also tend to suit different learning styles. These types are as follows:

- Microsoft Official Courses are for information technology (IT) professionals and developers who are new to a particular product or technology and for experienced individuals who prefer to learn in a traditional classroom format. Courses provide a relevant and guided learning experience that combines lecture and practice to deliver thorough coverage of a Microsoft product or technology. Courses are designed to address the needs of learners engaged in planning, design, implementation, management, and support phases of the technology adoption lifecycle. They provide detailed information by focusing on concepts and principles, reference content, and in-depth hands-on lab activities to ensure knowledge transfer. Typically, the content of a course is broad, addressing a wide range of tasks necessary for the job role.

- Microsoft Official Workshops are for knowledgeable IT professionals and developers who learn best by doing and exploring. Workshops provide a hands-on learning experience in which participants use Microsoft products in a safe and collaborative environment based on real-world scenarios. Workshops are the learning products where students learn by doing through scenario, and through troubleshooting hands-on labs, targeted reviews, information resources, and best practices, with instructor facilitation.

- Microsoft Official Clinics are for IT professionals, developers and technical decision makers. Clinics offer a detailed "how to" presentation that describes the features and functionality of an existing or new Microsoft product or technology, and that showcases product demonstrations and solutions. Clinics focus on how specific features will solve business problems.

- Microsoft Official Seminars are for business decision makers. Through featured business scenarios, case studies, and success stories, seminars provide a dynamic presentation of early and relevant information on Microsoft products and technology solutions that enable decision makers to make critical business decisions. Microsoft Official Seminars are concise, engaging, direct-from-the-source learning products that show how emerging Microsoft products and technologies help our customers serve their customers.

Microsoft Certified Professional Program

Microsoft Learning offers a variety of certification credentials for developers and IT professionals. The Microsoft Certified Professional (MCP) program is the leading certification program for validating your experience and skills, keeping you competitive in today's changing business environment.

MCP Certifications

The MCP program includes the following certifications.

- MCDST on Microsoft Windows XP

  The Microsoft Certified Desktop Support Technician (MCDST) certification is designed for professionals who successfully support and educate end users and troubleshoot operating system and application issues on desktop computers running the Windows operating system.

- MCSA on Microsoft Windows Server™ 2003

  The Microsoft Certified Systems Administrator (MCSA) certification is designed for professionals who implement, manage, and troubleshoot existing network and system environments based on the Windows Server 2003 platform. Implementation responsibilities include installing and configuring parts of systems. Management responsibilities include administering and supporting systems.

- MCSE on Windows Server 2003

  The Microsoft Certified Systems Engineer (MCSE) credential is the premier certification for professionals who analyze business requirements and design and implement infrastructure for business solutions based on the Windows Server 2003 platform. Implementation responsibilities include installing, configuring, and troubleshooting network systems.

- MCAD

  The Microsoft Certified Application Developer (MCAD) for Microsoft .NET credential is appropriate for professionals who use Microsoft technologies to develop and maintain department-level applications, components, Web or desktop clients, or back-end data services, or who work in teams developing enterprise applications. The credential covers job tasks ranging from developing to deploying and maintaining these solutions.

- MCSD

  The Microsoft Certified Solution Developer (MCSD) credential is the premier certification for professionals who design and develop leading-edge business solutions with Microsoft development tools, technologies, platforms, and the Microsoft Windows DNA architecture. The types of applications MCSDs can develop include desktop applications and multi-user, Web-based, N-tier, and transaction-based applications. The credential covers job tasks ranging from analyzing business requirements to maintaining solutions.

- MCDBA on Microsoft SQL Server 2000

  The Microsoft Certified Database Administrator (MCDBA) credential is the premier certification for professionals who implement and administer SQL Server databases. The certification is appropriate for individuals who derive physical database designs, develop logical data models, create physical databases, use Transact-SQL to create data services, manage and maintain databases, configure and manage security, monitor and optimize databases, and install and configure SQL Server.

- MCP

  The Microsoft Certified Professional (MCP) credential is for individuals who have the skills to successfully implement a Microsoft product or technology as part of a business solution in an organization. Hands-on experience with the product is necessary to successfully achieve certification.

- MCT

  Microsoft Certified Trainers (MCTs) demonstrate the instructional and technical skills that qualify them to deliver Official Microsoft Learning Products through a Microsoft Certified Partner for Learning Solutions.

Certification Requirements

Requirements differ for each certification category and are specific to the products and job functions addressed by the certification. To become a Microsoft Certified Professional, you must pass rigorous certification exams that provide a valid and reliable measure of technical proficiency and expertise.

 Additional Information See the Microsoft Learning Web site at http://www.microsoft.com/learning/.

You can also send e-mail to mcphelp@microsoft.com if you have specific certification questions.

Acquiring the Skills Tested by an MCP Exam

Official Microsoft Learning Products can help you develop the skills that you need to do your job. They also complement the experience that you gain while working with Microsoft products and technologies. However, no one-to-one correlation exists between Official Microsoft Learning Products and MCP exams. Microsoft does not expect or intend for a course or workshop to be the sole preparation method for passing MCP exams. Practical product knowledge and experience is also necessary to pass MCP exams.

To help prepare for MCP exams, use the preparation guides available for each exam. Each Exam Preparation Guide contains exam-specific information such as a list of topics on which you will be tested. These guides are available on the Microsoft Learning Web site at http://www.microsoft.com/learning/.

Facilities

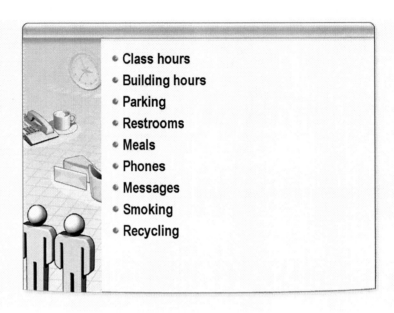

- Class hours
- Building hours
- Parking
- Restrooms
- Meals
- Phones
- Messages
- Smoking
- Recycling

Unit 1: Introduction to Visual Studio 2005

Contents

Information in this document, including URL and other Internet Web site references, is subject to change without notice. Unless otherwise noted, the example companies, organizations, products, domain names, e-mail addresses, logos, people, places, and events depicted herein are fictitious, and no association with any real company, organization, product, domain name, e-mail address, logo, person, place or event is intended or should be inferred. Complying with all applicable copyright laws is the responsibility of the user. Without limiting the rights under copyright, no part of this document may be reproduced, stored in or introduced into a retrieval system, or transmitted in any form or by any means (electronic, mechanical, photocopying, recording, or otherwise), or for any purpose, without the express written permission of Microsoft Corporation.

The names of manufacturers, products, or URLs are provided for informational purposes only and Microsoft makes no representations and warranties, either expressed, implied, or statutory, regarding these manufacturers or the use of the products with any Microsoft technologies. The inclusion of a manufacturer or product does not imply endorsement of Microsoft of the manufacturer or product. Links are provided to third party sites. Such sites are not under the control of Microsoft and Microsoft is not responsible for the contents of any linked site or any link contained in a linked site, or any changes or updates to such sites. Microsoft is not responsible for webcasting or any other form of transmission received from any linked site. Microsoft is providing these links to you only as a convenience, and the inclusion of any link does not imply endorsement of Microsoft of the site or the products contained therein.

Microsoft may have patents, patent applications, trademarks, copyrights, or other intellectual property rights covering subject matter in this document. Except as expressly provided in any written license agreement from Microsoft, the furnishing of this document does not give you any license to these patents, trademarks, copyrights, or other intellectual property.

© 2005 Microsoft Corporation. All rights reserved.

Microsoft, ActiveX, IntelliSense, MSDN, MS-DOS, PowerPoint, Visual Basic, Visual C#, Visual SourceSafe, Visual Studio, Visual Web Developer, Windows, Windows Media, Windows NT, and Windows Server are either registered trademarks or trademarks of Microsoft Corporation in the United States and/or other countries.

All other trademarks are property of their respective owners.

Overview

- The Visual Studio 2005 Product
- Productivity Enhancements In Visual Studio 2005
- Demonstration: Using the Lab Toolkit
- Lab: Programming Using Productivity Enhancements and Language Improvements

Objectives

After completing this unit, you will be able to:

- Identify the major new features in Microsoft® Visual Studio® 2005 that are addressed in this workshop.

- Identify the major productivity enhancements in Visual Studio 2005.

- Identify the tools and resources available to perform the tasks in this workshop.

The Visual Studio 2005 Product

- **Visual Studio 2005 Beta 2 supports development of applications for:**
  - .NET Framework
  - SQL Server 2005 Beta 2
  - .NET Compact Framework
- **The .NET Framework 2.0 contains major enhancements, including:**
  - ADO.NET 2.0
  - System.XML 2.0
  - Windows Forms 2.0
  - ASP.NET 2.0

Microsoft® Visual Studio® 2005 Beta 2 is a major new release of the comprehensive development environment for building Microsoft .NET–connected applications for Microsoft Windows® and the Web. This new version offers the following primary advantages:

- Radically improved developer productivity. Visual Studio 2005 contains integrated development environments (IDEs) for Microsoft Visual Basic®, Microsoft Visual C#®, and other programming languages, which include many features that make it faster and easier to develop software. These include edit marks, automatic saving of edits, improved rapid application development (RAD) features, and others. Visual Studio 2005 also contains improved graphical tools for specific application scenarios, such as Web page development and data access.

- Development of applications for .NET Framework 2.0.

- Development of applications that integrate with Microsoft SQL Server ™ 2005 Beta 2 or earlier versions of SQL Server, and development of managed code that runs inside of SQL Server 2005.

- Development of applications for handheld devices using .NET Compact Framework 2.0.

Microsoft .NET Framework 2.0 is the new version of the object-oriented programming environment used to develop applications ranging from traditional command-line or graphical user interface (GUI) applications to Web applications and Extensible Markup Language (XML) Web services. The .NET Framework 2.0 base class library (BCL) supports backward compatibility with earlier versions and also offers some enhancements to classes to perform common programming tasks such as string management, data collection, database connectivity, and file access. In addition to these common tasks, the BCL includes many enhancements to namespaces that support a variety of specialized development scenarios, including:

- ADO.NET 2.0, which consists of classes for efficient data access.

- System.XML 2.0, which consists of classes that enable you to read, write, manipulate, and transform XML.

- Windows Forms 2.0, which consists of classes to develop rich-client Windows GUI applications.

- Microsoft ASP.NET 2.0, which consists of classes to build Web applications and XML Web services.

Productivity Enhancements in Visual Studio 2005

- **Edit marks**
  - Green for recent edit, but saved
  - Yellow for unsaved
- **Code Snippets and code expansions**
  - Insert commonly used code
  - Easily create custom Snippets
- **C# productivity enhancements**
  - 'Edit and Continue' support
  - Automate common refactoring tasks
- **Visual Basic productivity enhancements**
  - 'Edit and Continue' support
  - Easy access to system and application resources with the MyServices abstraction

Software developers with experience with earlier versions of Visual Studio .NET will find many productivity enhancements in Visual Studio 2005.

Some of the most useful of these enhancements include:

- Edit marks

  Visual Studio 2005 provides you with a visual indication of what has changed during the editing session. It distinguishes between the changes you have made that have not yet been saved and changes you have made during the current session that have been saved to disk.

- Code Snippets

  Visual Studio 2005 includes a library of Code Snippets for common programming tasks. You can insert a Snippet into your code to achieve a programming task instead of searching the documentation or code samples for examples. You can also create your own Code Snippets.

- Visual C# productivity enhancements

  Visual Studio 2005 delivers a long-requested feature, which is the ability to correct programming errors during debugging and continue to run without restarting the program. The C# IDE includes a suite of tools that automate many common refactoring code tasks. Developers can easily rename classes, fields, properties, and methods, extract code into its own method, reorder or delete parameters to a method, promote a local variable to be a parameter, encapsulate fields, and perform many other refactoring tasks. The tools ensure that when any change is made, all dependant modules are also updated.

- Visual Basic productivity enhancements

  The Visual Basic IDE also includes the ability to edit code and continue to run without restarting the program. There are many other productivity enhancements, including the MyServices abstraction. MyServices is a series of coded shortcuts that make it easier to find system and application resources. For example, code such as My.Computer and My.WebServices are programmatic shortcuts to system resources and Web service references respectively.

Demonstration: Using the Lab Toolkit

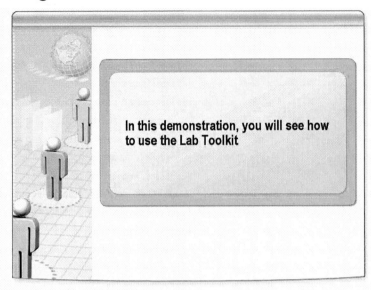

In this demonstration, you will see how you use the resources in the Lab Toolkit to help you to complete the lab exercises.

The Lab Toolkit has components like the:

1. Scenario tab:

    - Contains Technical specifications/Emails from the manager of Northwind Traders listed for that particular Lab.

    - Network Files: A shortcut to files referenced in labs.

2. Resources tab—Each unit will give you different Toolbox resources. A resource is a short article that provides details to complete a particular lab in addition to what is covered in the lecture.

Lab: Programming Using Productivity Enhancements and Language Improvements

In this lab, you will:

- Use the Lab Toolkit
- Reuse code using the Code Snippets feature
- Program strongly typed collections using generics

Visual C# developers will:

- Refactor code using the refactoring tools

Visual Basic developers will:

- Program with the My.* shortcuts to access application and system resources

After completing this lab, you will be able to:

- Use the Lab Toolkit.
- Reuse code using the Code Snippets feature.
- Program strongly typed collections using the **System.Collections.Generic** classes.

Visual C# developers will be able to:

- Refactor code using the refactoring tools.

Visual Basic developers will be able to:

- Program with the **My.*** shortcuts to access application and system resources.

 Important You can choose to program with either Visual C# or Visual Basic in this workshop. Code samples and lab solutions are provided in both programming languages. If you prefer, you can choose to perform some labs using one programming language, and perform others using the other language. However, once you start a lab, you should complete all the exercises in that lab using the same programming language. In the majority of labs in this workshop, the tasks you will perform are identical whether you choose to program in Visual C# or in Visual Basic. On rare occasions, such as in Lab 1, the tasks will be different, because of differing capabilities in the languages and tool support. Where such differences occur, the instructions will direct you to complete separate exercises for the lab following instructions for either Visual C# or Visual Basic.

Lab Setup

For this lab, you will use the LONDON UNIT 1 Virtual PC. Do not use the LONDON Virtual PC; that is for Units 2 through 6.

To prepare for this lab:

1. Start LONDON UNIT 1 Virtual PC.

2. Log on as **Student** with a password of **Pa$$w0rd**.

> **Best Practices** To improve security and minimize damage caused by mistakes, it is a good practice not to use an account with administrator privileges for your day-to-day use of a personal computer (PC) running Windows. This also applies to application development. The Student account used in this workshop does not have administrator privileges.

3. Click the **Labfiles** toolbar, which is located at the bottom right of the screen, and navigate to **Lab01\Setup**.

4. Click **Install** to set up the Virtual PC for this lab. This command file installs the starter code into Microsoft Visual SourceSafe® in preparation for the lab.

5. When prompted, enter the Administrators password, which is **Pa$$w0rd**.

6. Press any key to exit the setup command procedure.

Lab Toolkit Resources

Use the following Lab Toolkit Scenario and Resources to help you complete this lab:

- Northwind Traders Technical Specification: Suppliers Component Refactoring
- Importing and Exporting Visual Studio IDE Settings
- Using Code Snippets and Expansions to Automate the Creation of Common Code Constructs
- Refactoring Code Using Visual Studio 2005
- Programming with Generics
- Coding Standards at Northwind Traders

Estimated time to complete this lab: 75 minutes

Lab Solution Files

There are Visual Basic and Visual C# solution files associated with the labs in this workshop. The lab solution files are located in the folder E:\Microsoft Learning\2364\Labfiles\Lab01\Solution on the LONDON UNIT 1 Virtual PC.

Lab 1a: Instructions for Visual C# Programmers

 Important If you want to complete Unit 1 lab exercises using Visual C#, follow the instructions for Exercises 1 through 4. If you want to complete Unit 1 lab exercises using Visual Basic, turn to Lab 1b and begin the exercises there.

Exercise 1
Setting up Your Development Environment and Exploring the Lab Toolkit

In this exercise, you will set up Visual Studio 2005 according to your programming preferences. You will import code formatting settings that have been supplied by Nicole Holliday, a senior developer at Northwind Traders. You will also learn how to use the different components in the Lab Toolkit.

Scenario

You are a senior developer working for Northwind Traders. A new project called the Supplier Automated Reordering Project is beginning and will be built using Visual Studio 2005 and SQL Server 2005.

The first step is to set up Visual Studio 2005 for your preferred programming language, and to use the company-mandated code-formatting settings.

Tasks	Supporting information
1. Open the Lab Toolkit and review its contents.	See the resource in the Lab Toolkit, *Using the Lab Toolkit*. ▪ You can access the Lab Toolkit by double-clicking the icon on your desktop. ▪ As you work through each step in the lab exercise (in addition to offering tips and advice on best practices), the Supporting Information column will recommend resources to help you. For example, if you aren't sure how to import IDE settings in Visual Studio 2005, you can use a resource listed on the Resources tab in the Lab Toolkit. If you already know what to do, you don't need to use the resource. ▪ Sometimes, the same resource will be recommended for similar tasks.
2. Start Visual Studio 2005, and when prompted, choose the initial IDE settings of Visual C# Development Settings.	See the resource in the Lab Toolkit, *Importing and Exporting Visual Studio IDE Settings*. ▪ The first time you start Visual Studio 2005, you must select your preferred programming settings. Settings control features such as key mappings to Visual Studio .NET functions, the layout of the New Programs window, and formatting of code in the code editor. ▪ You can change your settings at a later time by importing the default settings for a different programming language, or by importing custom settings that you create.

(continued)

Tasks	Supporting information
3. Read the e-mail from Nicole Holliday and import the Visual C# settings, NorthwindVCS.vssettings.	See the following resources in the Lab Toolkit: ■ The e-mail, *Coding Standards at Northwind Traders* ■ *Importing and Exporting Visual Studio IDE Settings* ■ The e-mail states that the settings files are in the Network Files folder. See the Lab Toolkit for access to the Network Files folder. ■ Import the Visual C# language settings, NorthwindVCS.vssettings. ■ There are two differences in the NorthwindVCS.vssettings file from the initial settings you had chosen: • Keywords in the Source Code Editor are colored blue. • Line Numbering has been switched on. ■ On the **Tools** menu, click **Options** to view other settings.

Exercise 2
Reusing Code Using the Code Snippets Feature

In this exercise, you will open a solution that was created in Visual Studio .NET 2003 and convert it for use in Visual Studio 2005. You will reformat the code and create a snippet for a standard header that you place at the top of every code module.

Scenario

The Automated Supplier Reordering project will use some existing code created for earlier Northwind Traders projects. However, new coding standards have been adopted by the company since the code was written, so before the existing code modules must be upgraded before they can be used again.

The first stage in upgrading the existing code modules is to ensure that each code module is correctly formatted and includes the standard company header.

Tasks	Supporting information
1. Load the Supplier solution and perform the conversion.	■ On the **File** menu, point to **Open**, and then click **Project/Solution**.
	■ Click the **My SourceSafe (LAN)** icon to look for the project.
	■ Click **Add SourceSafe Database**, and then click **Open** to start the Add SourceSafe Database Wizard.
	■ Click **Next** on the welcome screen of the wizard. Select **Connect using the network at my workplace** for the Database connection type, and then click **Next**. Type **C:\SourcesafeDB** as the location, and then click **Next**. Enter a friendly name for the Sourcesafe database, such as **NorthwindSourcesafe**, and then click **Next**. Click **Finish**.
	■ After the Add SourceSafe Database Wizard completes, select the database you just added in the Open Project window, and then click **Open**.
	■ In the Log on to Visual SourceSafe Database window, type the user name **Student**, leave the password field blank, and then click **OK**.
	■ Open the solution from 2364\Unit01\CS\Supplier.
	■ Run the Visual Studio Conversion Wizard to convert the solution to Visual Studio 2005 format.
	■ Compile and run the solution in the debugger to ensure that it works, and to familiarize yourself with how the application operates. You may need to go to Solution Explorer and set the **SupplierTestApp** project as the Startup project.
	■ There will be an error when you run the program. You will correct this in the next step.
	• Notice that a window appears that is titled ArgumentException was unhandled. This window is part of a new feature of Visual Studio 2005 that gives you more information when you get unhandled exceptions during debugging.
	• Click the **View Detail** link to find out more about the run-time error.

(continued)

Tasks	Supporting information
2. Correct any compilation or run-time errors.	▪ .NET Framework 2.0 supports backward compatibility for applications developed using earlier versions. However, sometimes .NET Framework 2.0 is stricter about certain syntax than earlier versions, which can lead to breaking of older code. ▪ The SupplierTestApp application fails with a run-time error because the code in the **Form1** constructor assigns a value to the **DataSource** property and then sets the **Sorted** property of the ComboBox to **true**, which is not allowed. ▪ Modify the code to set the **Sorted** property of the ComboBox to **false** to correct the run-time error. **Visual C# New Feature** Visual Studio 2005 includes Edit and Continue, to allow you to change the code during debugging, recompile dynamically, and continue debugging without restarting the application. Try this now.
3. Review the existing solution code.	▪ Before making any modifications, review the existing code to understand what it does and how it works. Examine the following files: • Supplier.cs • SupplierComponent.cs • SupplierDB.cs • SupplierList.cs • Form1.cs ▪ Based on the technical specification, identify the areas that need to be refactored and enhanced. See the resource in the Lab Toolkit, *Northwind Traders Technical Specification: Suppliers Component Refactoring*.
4. Reformat all code.	▪ The standard format settings for Northwind Traders are contained in the profile you loaded into Visual Studio 2005 in Exercise 1. ▪ Open each of the source files listed earlier, and, from the **Edit** menu, click **Advanced**, and then click **Format Document**.
5. Read the e-mail from Nicole Holliday again and implement standard file headers using Visual Studio 2005's Code Snippets feature.	See the e-mail resource in the Lab Toolkit, *Coding Standards at Northwind Traders*. ▪ The second part of the e-mail from the lead developer described a standard header that must be applied to all source files. ▪ Copy the standard header from the e-mail, and paste it in the top of the Supplier.cs file, just below the **using** statements. ▪ You see that the standard file header contains information that is unique for each file, including: • The creation date • The initial author • The summary description

(continued)

Tasks	Supporting information
6. Add the development group snippets folder to Visual Studio by using the Code Snippets Manager.	See the resource in the Lab Toolkit, *Using Code Snippets to Automate the Creation of Common Code Constructs.* ■ The Northwind Traders development group has created a snippet to simplify the process of adding a header to a class file. This snippet is located in the network folder named E:\Network files\Visual Studio Code Snippets\Visual C#\Northwind. Open the snippet file in this folder and examine its structure. Close the file when finished. ■ On the **Tools** menu, click **Code Snippets Manager**. Add the Northwind folder from E:\Network Files\Visual Studio Code Snippets\Visual C# to the list of recognized snippet folders for Visual C#.
7. Apply the standard header to all files.	■ Just below the **using** statements, right-click on an empty line. ■ Select **Insert Snippet**, click **Northwind**, and then select the **Standard Class File Header** snippet. ■ Replace the values in the highlighted placeholder.
8. Compile and run the code.	■ Having made significant changes to the structure of the code, compile and run the solution to make sure it still works before proceeding.

Exercise 3
Visual C# Refactoring

In this exercise, you will continue to transform the Supplier solution to conform to company coding standards. You have already addressed the structure of the code, but the coding standards also specify best practices for the naming of class members, fields, properties, and methods. This is an area in which the existing Supplier solution requires significant amounts of work. Without the refactoring features of Visual Studio 2005, this work would be error-prone and time-consuming.

 Important This exercise covers the use of new tools for refactoring in the Visual C# IDE in Visual Studio 2005.

It is possible for Visual Basic developers to carry out similar tasks in their applications, but the coding must be done manually, because the Visual Basic IDE provides only a Rename tool, and there are no other refactoring tools built in to make the job easier.

Scenario

The Automated Supplier Reordering project will use some existing code created for earlier Northwind Traders projects. However, new coding standards have been adopted by the company since the code was written, so the existing code modules must be upgraded before they can be used again.

The second stage in upgrading the existing code modules is to ensure that class members are named in accordance with company standards, and that public properties use **get/set** accessors.

Tasks	Supporting information
1. Convert a field to a property.	See the resource in the Lab Toolkit, *Refactoring Code Using Visual Studio 2005*.
	▪ The **Supplier** class (Supplier.cs) already contains two methods, **validatePhoneNumber** and **validateFaxNumber**, that are used to validate input when calling the **Supplier** constructor. However, these methods are currently not used when setting either the public **o_Fax** or **o_Phone** fields.
	▪ Change these two fields to be public properties:
	• The properties should have **get** and **set** accessors. Use the Encapsulate Field refactoring tool to achieve this.
	• Use the Rename tool to store the value in a private field called _fax for the **Fax** property and_phone for the **Phone** property.
	▪ Call the **validatePhoneNumber** method in the **set** accessor of the **Phone** property to validate input. If **validatePhoneNumber** returns **true**, set the _phone field with the input value; otherwise throw an **ArgumentException**.
	▪ Program similar validation on the **set** accessor of the **Fax** property by calling the **validateFaxNumber** method.

(*continued*)

Tasks	Supporting information
2. Convert the remaining fields to properties.	▪ Convert all the remaining fields so that they conform to company naming conventions: • Each public data member is accessed through a public property and the name is capitalized. • Each property stores its value in a private field that uses camel casing and starts with an underscore '_'.
3. Set accessibility on property accessors.	▪ .NET Framework 2.0 supports accessibility settings on individual property accessors. ▪ For example, you can write a property with **get** and **set** accessors, and set the **get** accessor to public and the **set** accessor to private. This restricts the **set** accessor to use solely by code in the same class. ▪ Do this now. Change the **SupplierID** public property. Set the **set** accessor to **private**. Leave the **get** accessor as is; it will default to being **public**.
4. Insert #region directives.	▪ The code for the private fields and public properties is now very large. The Supplier.cs code module is easier to work with if the code is in its own region, which may be collapsed or expanded, as required. ▪ Select all the code for the properties. Right-click on the code and click **Surround with**, click **Visual C#** and then click **#region**. ▪ Repeat for the constructor and for the static methods in the class.
5. Extract the interface.	See the following resources in the Lab Toolkit: ▪ *Refactoring Code Using Visual Studio 2005* ▪ *Northwind Traders Technical Specification: Suppliers Component Refactoring* ▪ The team has decided that the supplier information would be best represented by an interface named **ISupplier**. This allows a number of different supplier classes to be developed, all of which implement the basic requirements of a supplier object as described by the **ISupplier** interface. ▪ Right-click anywhere in the **Supplier** class, point to **Refactoring**, and then, from the shortcut menu, click **Extract Interface**. ▪ Note that the system provided the name **ISupplier** for the interface and the name **ISupplier.cs** for the file name. Use these default values, and include all properties in the new interface. ▪ Change the namespace of the generated file to **NorthwindTraders**. ▪ The refactoring tools modified the class declaration to state that it implements **Supplier.ISupplier**. You will therefore need to change the Supplier class in **Supplier.cs** to **NorthwindTraders.ISupplier**.

(continued)

Tasks	Supporting information
6. Rename the Supplier Class.	See the resource in the Lab Toolkit, *Refactoring Code Using Visual Studio 2005*. ■ The **Supplier** class is now just one of many classes that could potentially implement **ISupplier**. To make this clearer, use the refactoring tool to rename it to **SupplierBase**.
7. Extract a method.	See the resource in the Lab Toolkit, *Refactoring Code Using Visual Studio 2005*. ■ Open the module SupplierComponent.cs and find the static method **GetSuppliersByCountry**. ■ Make this method more readable by extracting all the code in the **foreach** statement into a separate method. ■ Name the method **AddNewSupplier**.
8. Compile and run the code.	■ Compile and run the solution.

Exercise 4 (Optional)
Programming Strongly Typed Collections Using Generics

In this exercise, which you should perform if you have time, you will use generics, an important new feature of the .NET Framework 2.0 Common Language Runtime (CLR) to simplify the Supplier solution. Specifically, you will replace the custom **SupplierList** with one of the new collection classes in the **System.Collections.Generic** namespace.

Scenario

The Supplier library contains a class called **SupplierList** that implements a strongly typed collection of supplier objects. A technical review has identified that performance will be improved and unnecessary code removed by using a **List<T>** class, one of the generic collection classes implemented in the .NET Framework 2.0.

Tasks	Supporting information
1. Review SupplierList.cs.	▪ The **SupplierList** class is a strongly typed list of **Supplier** objects that extends **CollectionBase**. With generics, you will not need this custom class.
2. Identify places where the **SupplierList** class is used.	▪ Use a new feature of Visual Studio 2005 that allows you to find all references to a symbolic variable.
	▪ Right-click **SupplierList** in the class declaration in SupplierList.cs and click **Find All References**.
	▪ The Find Symbol Results window lists all references to the class in your solution. Right-click any line in this window and click **Go To Reference** to view the code where the reference to **SupplierList** is located.
3. Remove **SupplierList**.	▪ Fix **SupplierComponent.cs** and **Form1.cs**. Use the list of references in the Find Symbol Results window to locate references to the **SupplierList** class in these code modules.
| | 💡 **Tip** Change all references to **SupplierList** to **System.Collections.Generic.List<SupplierBase>**. For example, change the method signature of the **GetSuppliersByCountry** static method in SupplierComponent.cs to the following, and then make other necessary code changes:<br><br>```csharp
public static
System.Collections.Generic.List<SupplierBase>
GetSuppliersByCountry (String country)
```<br><br>▪ Delete the SupplierList.cs file. |
| 4. Compile and run the code. | ▪ All aspects of refactoring and enhancing the code are complete. Compile and run the solution. |
```

Lab 1b: Instructions for Visual Basic Programmers

 Important If you want to complete Unit 1 lab exercises using Visual Basic, perform the following Exercises 1 to 4. If you want to complete Unit 1 lab exercises using Visual C#, turn back to Lab 1a and follow the exercises there.

Exercise 1
Setting Up Your Development Environment and Exploring the Lab Toolkit

In this exercise, you will set up Visual Studio 2005 according to your programming references. You will import code-formatting settings that have been supplied by Nicole Holliday, senior developer at Northwind Traders. You will also learn how to use the different components in the Lab Toolkit.

Scenario

You are a senior developer working for Northwind Traders. A new project called the Supplier Automated Reordering Project is beginning and will be built using Visual Studio 2005 and SQL Server 2005.

The first step is to set up Visual Studio 2005 for your preferred programming language and to use the company-mandated code-formatting settings.

Tasks	Supporting information
1. Open the Lab Toolkit and review its contents.	See the resource in the Lab Toolkit, *Using the Lab Toolkit.* ■ You can access the Lab Toolkit by double-clicking the icon on your desktop. ■ As you work through each step in the lab exercise (in addition to offering tips and advice on best practices), the Supporting Information column will recommend resources to help you. For example, if you aren't sure how to import IDE settings in Visual Studio 2005, you can use a resource listed on the Resources tab in the Lab Toolkit. If you already know what to do, you don't need to use the resource. ■ Sometimes the same resource will be recommended for similar tasks.
2. Start Visual Studio 2005 and when prompted, choose the initial IDE settings of Visual Basic Development Settings.	See the resource in the Lab Toolkit, *Importing and Exporting Visual Studio IDE Settings.* ■ The first time you start Visual Studio 2005, you must select your preferred programming settings. Settings control features such as key mappings to Visual Studio .NET functions, the layout of the New Programs window, and formatting of code in the code editor. ■ You can change your settings at a later time by importing the default settings for a different programming language, or by importing custom settings that you create.

(*continued*)

Tasks	Supporting information

3. Read the e-mail from Nicole Holliday and import the Visual Basic settings, NorthwindVB.vssettings.	See the following resources in the Lab Toolkit:
	
	• The e-mail, *Coding Standards at Northwind Traders*
	
	• *Importing and Exporting Visual Studio IDE Settings*
	
	• The e-mail states that the settings files are in the Network Files folder. See the Lab Toolkit for access to the Network Files folder.
	
	• Import the Visual Basic language settings, NorthwindVB.vssettings.
	
	• There are two differences in the NorthwindVB.vssettings file from the initial settings you have chosen:
	
	  • Keywords in the Source Code Editor are colored blue.
	
	  • Option Strict has been switched on.
	
	• From the **Tools** menu, click **Options** to view other settings.

Exercise 2
Reusing Code Using the Code Snippets Feature

In this exercise, you will open a solution that was created in Visual Studio .NET 2003 and convert it for use in Visual Studio 2005. You will reformat the code and create a snippet for a standard header that you place at the top of every code module.

Scenario

The Automated Supplier Reordering project will use some existing code created for earlier Northwind Traders projects. However, new coding standards have been adopted by the company since the code was written, so the existing code modules must be upgraded before they can be used again.

The first stage in upgrading the existing code modules is to ensure that each code module is correctly formatted and includes the standard company header.

Tasks	Supporting information
1. Load the Supplier solution and perform conversion.	■ On the **File** menu, point to **Open**, and then click **Project/Solution**. ■ Click the **My SourceSafe** icon to look for the project. ■ Double-click **Add SourceSafe Database** to start the Add SourceSafe Database Wizard. ■ On the **Welcome** page of the wizard, click **Next**. Select **Connect using the network at my workplace** for the Database connection type, and then click **Next**. Type **C:\SourcesafeDB** as the location, and then click **Next**. Enter a friendly name for the SourceSafe database, such as **NorthwindSourcesafe**, click **Next**, and then click **Finish**. ■ After the Add SourceSafe Database wizard completes, select the database you just added in the **Open Project** window, then click **Open**. ■ In the Visual SourceSafe Login window, type the user name **Student**, leave the password field blank, and then click **OK**. ■ Open the solution from 2364\Unit01\VB\Supplier. ■ Run the Visual Studio Conversion Wizard to convert the solution to Visual Studio 2005 format.

2. Run the application in debug mode.	■ Compile and run the solution in the debugger to ensure that it works and to familiarize yourself with how the application operates. You may need to go to Solution Explorer and set the SupplierTestApp project as the Startup project.
	
	■ There will be an error when you run the program. You will correct this in the next step.
	
	    • Notice that a window appears titled ArgumentException was unhandled. This window is a new feature of Visual Studio 2005 that gives you more information when you get unhandled exceptions during debugging.
	
	    • Click the **View Detail** link to find out more about the run-time error.

(continued)

Tasks	Supporting information
3. Correct any compilation or run-time errors.	**Important** Before running the program, open Form1.vb in the code view. In this step, you will try out Visual Basic Edit and Continue, but Visual Studio 2005 Beta 2 allows editing during debugging only if the file is open in code view.
	■ The .NET Framework 2.0 supports backward compatibility for applications developed using earlier versions. However, sometimes .NET Framework 2.0 is stricter about certain syntax than earlier versions, which can lead to the breaking of older code.
	■ The SupplierTestApp application fails with a run-time error because the code in the **Form1** constructor assigns a value to the **DataSource** property and then sets the **Sorted** property of the ComboBox to **true**, which is not allowed.
	■ Modify the code to set the **Sorted** property of the ComboBox to **false** to correct the run-time error.
	Visual Basic New Feature Visual Studio 2005 includes Edit and Continue to allow you to change code during debugging, recompile dynamically, and continue debugging without restarting the application. Try this now.
4. Review the existing solution code.	See the resource in the Lab Toolkit, *Northwind Traders Technical Specification: Suppliers Component Refactoring*.
	■ Before making any modifications, review the existing code to understand what it does and how it works. Examine the following files:
	• Supplier.vb
	• SupplierComponent.vb
	• SupplierDB.vb
	• SupplierList.vb
	• Form1.vb
	■ Based on the technical specification, identify the areas that need to be refactored and enhanced.
5. Reformat all code.	■ The standard format settings for Northwind Traders are contained in the profile you loaded into Visual Studio 2005 in Exercise 1.
	■ Open each source file and on the **Edit** menu, click **Advanced**, and then click **Format Document**.

(continued)

Tasks	Supporting information
6. Read the e-mail from Nicole Holliday again and implement standard file headers using Visual Studio 2005's Code Snippets feature.	See the e-mail resource in the Lab Toolkit, *Coding Standards at Northwind Traders*. ▪ The second part of the e-mail from the lead developer described a standard header that must be applied to all source files. ▪ Copy the standard header from the e-mail, select the text, and then paste it in the top of the Supplier.vb file, just below the **Imports** statement. ▪ You see that the standard file header contains information that is unique for each file, including: • The creation date • The initial author • The summary description
7. Add the development group snippets folder to Visual Studio using the Code Snippets Manager.	See the resource in the Lab Toolkit, *Using Code Snippets and Expansions to Automate the Creation of Common Code Constructs*. ▪ The Northwind Traders development group has created a snippet to simplify the process of adding a header to a class file. This snippet is located in the network folder named \\london\network files\Visual Studio Code Snippets\Visual Basic\Northwind. Open the snippet file in this folder and examine its structure. Close the file when finished. ▪ On the **Tools** menu, click **Code Snippets Manager**. Add the Northwind folder from E:\Network Files\Visual Studio Code Snippets\Visual Basic to the list of recognized snippet folders for Visual Basic.
8. Apply the standard header to all files.	▪ Point on an empty line, just below the **Imports** statements. ▪ Right-click next to the pointer, select **Insert Snippet**, click **Northwind**, and then select the **Standard Class File Header** snippet. ▪ Replace the values in the highlighted placeholder.
9. Compile and run the code.	▪ Having made significant changes to the structure of the code, compile and run the solution to make sure it still works before proceeding.

Exercise 3
Visual Basic MyServices

In this exercise, you will continue to transform the Supplier solution to conform to company coding standards. The next stage is to move the database connection setting into a Settings file and to modify the code to use it.

Important This exercise makes use of new features in the Visual Basic IDE in Visual Studio 2005. It is possible for Visual C# developers to add similar functionality to their applications, but the coding must be done manually because no language extensions or tools are built into the Visual C# IDE to make the job easier.

Scenario

The Supplier Library contains a class named **SupplierDB**, which contains code that interacts with the database. The database connection string is currently hard-coded in the module but should be removed to a settings file for easier modification after deployment.

Tasks	Supporting information
1. Review SupplierDB.vb.	See the resource in the Lab Toolkit, *Northwind Traders Technical Specification: Suppliers Component Refactoring*. ■ In this exercise, you will move the database connection string to an application settings file, which is one of the requirements listed in the Technical Specification.
2. Open Project Properties.	■ In Solution Explorer, right-click the **Supplier** project, and then click **Properties**. This opens the new **Project Designer**, which is a new tool for managing all the settings and references for your application. Notice that Visual Studio 2005 added an item to the Supplier project called My Project when you converted the project at the beginning of this lab. ■ You can open the Project Designer in two ways: you can right-click **My Project** and then click **Open**, or you can open the project properties as just described.
3. Move the database connection string to the Settings file.	■ Click the **Settings** tab, and then add an item named **ConnectionString** into the grid, using the value currently hard-coded in SupplierDB.vb.
4. Modify SupplierDB.vb to read the connection string from the settings file.	■ Delete the hard-coded connection string in SupplierDB.vb, and then type **My** followed by a dot (.). Use IntelliSense® to see how to retrieve the **ConnectionString** item from the settings file. ■ Visual Basic MyServices is an abstraction layer that makes it easy to access commonly used .NET Framework classes, systems, and application resources. You can also access My.Computer, My.Application, My.WebServices, and My.User. You will be able to experiment with many of these features during the remainder of this course.
5. Compile and run the code.	■ Compile and run the solution.

Exercise 4 (Optional)
Programming Strongly Typed Collections Using Generics

In this exercise, which you should perform if you have time, you will use generics, an important new feature of the .NET Framework 2.0 Common Language Runtime (CLR) to simplify the Supplier solution. Specifically, you will replace the custom **SupplierList** with one of the new collection classes in the **System.Collections.Generic** namespace.

Scenario

The Supplier Library contains a class named **SupplierList** that implements a strongly typed collection of Supplier objects. A technical review has identified that performance will be improved and unnecessary code removed by using a **List<T>** class, one of the generic collection classes implemented in the .NET Framework 2.0.

Tasks	Supporting information
1. Review SupplierList.vb.	▪ The **SupplierList** class is a strongly typed list of Supplier objects that extends **CollectionBase**. With generics, you will not need this class.
2. Identify places where the **SupplierList** class is used.	▪ Use a new feature of Visual Studio 2005 that allows you to find all references to a symbolic variable. Right-click **SupplierList** in the class declaration in SupplierList.vb, and then click **Find all References**.
	▪ The Find Symbol Results window lists all references to the class in your solution. Right-click any line in this window, and click **Go To Reference** to view the code where the reference to **SupplierList** is located. Alternatively, try double-clicking the reference.
3. Remove **SupplierList**.	▪ Fix **SupplierComponent.vb** and **Form1.vb**. Use the list of references in the Find Symbol Results window to locate references to the **SupplierList** class in these code modules.
	Tip Change all references to **SupplierList** to **System.Collections.Generic.List(Of Supplier)**. For example, change the method signature of the **GetSuppliersByCountry** static method in SupplierComponent.vb to the following, and then make other necessary code changes: `Public Shared Function GetSuppliersByCountry(ByVal country As String) As System.Collections.Generic.List(Of Supplier)`.
	▪ Delete the SupplierList.vb file.
4. Compile and run the code.	▪ All aspects of refactoring and enhancing the code are complete. Compile and run the solution.

Lab Discussion

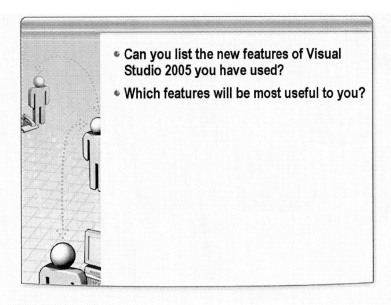

You have experienced many new features of Visual Studio 2005 in this first lab. Work with the class to see if you can list all the new features that you encountered, including any you discovered that were not specifically highlighted by the lab activities.

Discuss with the class which of the new features will be most useful and will allow you to develop software more productively.

Unit 2: Building Managed Code for SQL Server 2005

Contents

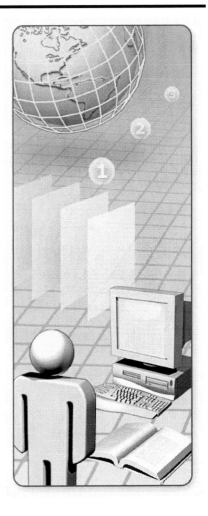

Information in this document, including URL and other Internet Web site references, is subject to change without notice. Unless otherwise noted, the example companies, organizations, products, domain names, e-mail addresses, logos, people, places, and events depicted herein are fictitious, and no association with any real company, organization, product, domain name, e-mail address, logo, person, place or event is intended or should be inferred. Complying with all applicable copyright laws is the responsibility of the user. Without limiting the rights under copyright, no part of this document may be reproduced, stored in or introduced into a retrieval system, or transmitted in any form or by any means (electronic, mechanical, photocopying, recording, or otherwise), or for any purpose, without the express written permission of Microsoft Corporation.

The names of manufacturers, products, or URLs are provided for informational purposes only and Microsoft makes no representations and warranties, either expressed, implied, or statutory, regarding these manufacturers or the use of the products with any Microsoft technologies. The inclusion of a manufacturer or product does not imply endorsement of Microsoft of the manufacturer or product. Links are provided to third party sites. Such sites are not under the control of Microsoft and Microsoft is not responsible for the contents of any linked site or any link contained in a linked site, or any changes or updates to such sites. Microsoft is not responsible for webcasting or any other form of transmission received from any linked site. Microsoft is providing these links to you only as a convenience, and the inclusion of any link does not imply endorsement of Microsoft of the site or the products contained therein.

Microsoft may have patents, patent applications, trademarks, copyrights, or other intellectual property rights covering subject matter in this document. Except as expressly provided in any written license agreement from Microsoft, the furnishing of this document does not give you any license to these patents, trademarks, copyrights, or other intellectual property.

© 2005 Microsoft Corporation. All rights reserved.

Microsoft, ActiveX, IntelliSense, MSDN, MS-DOS, PowerPoint, Visual Basic, Visual C#, Visual SourceSafe, Visual Studio, Visual Web Developer, Windows, Windows Media, Windows NT, and Windows Server are either registered trademarks or trademarks of Microsoft Corporation in the United States and/or other countries.

All other trademarks are property of their respective owners.

Overview

- CLR Integration with SQL Server 2005
- SQL Server Projects in Visual Studio 2005
- Demonstration: Creating a UDT in Managed Code
- Lab 2A: Writing Managed Code for SQL Server 2005
- Lab 2B: Working with XML in Visual Studio 2005 and SQL Server 2005

To help control access to data, preserve data integrity, and improve productivity, software developers must often write reusable sets of Transact-SQL code to be stored in the database. Microsoft® SQL Server™ 2005 supports the use of managed code to write stored procedures, user-defined types (UDTs), user-defined functions, and triggers, which allow the full power of the .NET Framework to be used, instead of the more limited Transact-SQL. Also, many developers are using Extensible Markup Language (XML) and related technologies to represent and manipulate data. Microsoft SQL Server 2005 provides enhanced support for storing and manipulating XML. Microsoft Visual Studio® 2005 provides new tools (such as the Schema Designer) and new XML objects that help developers work with XML data.

Objectives

After completing this unit, you will be able to:

- Create a managed assembly to run inside SQL Server 2005.

- Create a managed user-defined function.

- Create a managed stored procedure.

- Create a managed user-defined type (UDT), store it in a SQL Server table, and use it in a program.

- Create an XML schema using the Visual Studio 2005 XML Designer.

- Create XML columns in SQL Server databases.

- Add XML data to XML columns.

- Create XML schemas.

- Publish XML schemas so that they can be accessed both programmatically and manually.

- Validate XML documents using schemas.

- Process and query XML data using .NET classes.

CLR Integration with SQL Server 2005

* Run managed code within a database by using in-process assemblies

* Create managed stored procedures, triggers, user- defined functions, user- defined types, and aggregates

* Integration benefits:
    * Enhanced programming model
    * Enhanced safety and security
    * Common development environment
    * Performance and scalability

SQL Server 2005 integrates the Common Language Runtime (CLR) into the database. This integration provides you with considerable flexibility when designing your database application.

Managed Code

The integration of the CLR into SQL Server 2005 allows you to run managed code directly within a database. In its most basic form, this is a similar concept to calling extended stored procedures in earlier versions of SQL Server. However, the CLR integration provides much more power and flexibility than traditional extended stored procedures.

Managed SQL Server Objects

CLR integration allows you to create database objects including stored procedures, triggers, user-defined functions, UDTs, and aggregates, in any .NET language. You can use these database objects directly from your SQL Server 2005 databases as you would use any other database object.

Integration Benefits

CLR integration in SQL Server 2005 provides you with many benefits including:

* *Enhanced programming model.* The .NET Framework languages offer richer development capabilities than Transact-SQL.

* *Enhanced safety and security.* Managed code runs in a CLR environment hosted by the SQL Server database engine. This provides a safer and more secure system than extended stored procedures.

* *Common development environment.* You use the same tools for developing and debugging database objects and scripts as developers use to write .NET Framework components and applications.

* *Performance and scalability.* Managed code and managed execution can, in many situations, deliver improved performance over Transact-SQL.

SQL Server Projects in Visual Studio 2005

- Project for creating managed database objects
- Automatically includes necessary references
  - sqlaccess.dll
  - System.Data.dll
- Includes templates for each object type
- Allows immediate deployment and debugging

Visual Studio 2005 includes a new project type that allows you to create and deploy managed database objects with SQL Server 2005.

Create SQL Server Project for Managed Code

This new SQL Server project type allows you to create managed database objects within Visual Studio 2005. This type of project creates an in-process assembly (a class library) as required for SQL Server 2005 CLR integration.

When you create a SQL Server project, Visual Studio 2005 prompts you to select an existing SQL Server connection defined in Solution Explorer, or to create a new connection. This connection is used to deploy your solution from Visual Studio 2005.

Automatic References

To create and test managed database objects, you need to use the following managed assemblies:

- **sqlaccess.dll**
  Provides the necessary objects to allow your managed code to access database objects such as tables and views

- **System.Data.dll**
  Provides additional objects and attributes for creating managed database objects, as well as the standard ADO.NET 2.0 classes

 Additional Information Information about some of the classes found in the sqlaccess assembly is included in the Toolkit resource, Using the Microsoft.SqlServer.Server Namespace.

The SQL Server project template automatically references these assemblies whenever you create a project based on the template.

Object Templates

The SQL Server project provides templates for creating all the managed database objects, such as stored procedures, user-defined functions, and UDTs. You can also add standard managed class files to your project.

Visual Studio 2005 adds a file named Test.sql to a TestScripts folder in the project when you add the first managed database object to the project. This file contains a statement that executes the newly created managed database object.

Immediate Deployment and Debugging

The SQL Server project allows you to deploy your managed database objects with a single mouse click. The **Build** menu contains a **Deploy Project** command that, when run, compiles your assembly and registers it with SQL Server 2005.

Visual Studio 2005 executes the Test.sql file when you run your project, allowing you to step through your managed code. You can use traditional debugging techniques such as setting breakpoints within your code and taking advantage of the various debugger windows that display useful information.

Demonstration: Creating a UDT in Managed Code

In this demonstration, you will see how to create a UDT in managed code and deploy it to SQL Server 2005. The instructor will:

1. Create a SQL Server Project.

2. Create a simple UDT.

3. Build and deploy the managed code.

4. Debug the UDT using a Transact-SQL script within Visual Studio .NET 2005.

Lab 2A: Writing Managed Code for SQL Server 2005

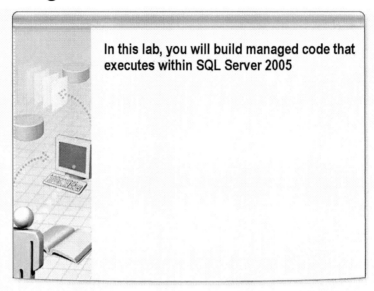

In this lab, you will build managed code that executes within SQL Server 2005

After completing this lab, you will be able to:

- Create a managed assembly to run inside SQL Server 2005.
- Create a managed user-defined function.
- Create a managed stored procedure.
- Create a managed UDT, store it in a SQL Server table, and use it in a program.

 Important If you need to redeploy the managed assembly to SQL server 2005 more than once, you must run CleanUpVB.cmd or CleanUpCS.cmd located in the E:\Microsoft Learning\ 2364\Labfiles\Lab02a folder. This script removes the managed code from SQL Server 2005 so that you can cleanly redeploy a new version.

Lab Setup

For this lab, you will use the LONDON Virtual PC.

To prepare for this lab:

1. If LONDON UNIT 1 Virtual PC is still running after the previous lab, on the **Action** menu, click **Close**. The **Action** menu is visible when the Virtual PC is running in windowed mode, but not when it is running full screen. If you are running the Virtual PC full screen, press <RIGHT>ALT+ ENTER to switch back to windowed mode.

   In the Close window, select **Turn off and delete changes** and then click **OK**.

2. Start the LONDON Virtual PC. Do not use the LONDON UNIT 1 Virtual PC that you used in Unit 1.

3. Log on as **Student** with a password of **Pa$$w0rd**.

4. Click the **Labfiles** toolbar, located at the bottom right of the screen and navigate to **Lab02a\Setup**.

5. Click **Install** to set up the Virtual PC for this lab. This command file sets up database security to allow the Student account to deploy to SQL Server.

6. Enter the Administrator's password when prompted, which is **Pa$$w0rd**.

7. Press any key to exit the setup command procedure.

 Caution The setup procedure for this lab performs operations with the SQL Server. If you have recently started the virtual PC, the database server may not have completed its startup. If you run the install script and you see either of the following errors, wait a few minutes and then try to run the install script again:

- Client unable to establish connection
- Shared Memory Provider: The system cannot find the file specified.
- Timeout expired.

Lab Toolkit Resources

If necessary, use one or more of the following Lab Toolkit resources to help you complete this lab:

- Northwind Traders Technical Specification: NorthwindSQL Class Library.
- Using the **Microsoft.SqlServer.Server** namespace.
- Creating Stored Procedures in Managed Code.
- Creating a User-Defined Function in Managed Code.
- Creating a User-Defined Type in Managed Code.
- Debugging and Deploying Managed Code to SQL Server 2005.

Estimated time to complete this lab: **75 minutes**

Lab Solution Files

There are Microsoft Visual Basic® and Microsoft Visual C#® solution files associated with the labs in this workshop. The lab solution files are located in the folder E:\Microsoft Learning\2364\ Labfiles\Lab02a\Solution on the Virtual PCs.

Follow the following steps to run one of the supplied solutions:

1. Log on as **Administrator** with a password of **Pa$$w0rd**.

2. Start Windows Explorer, and navigate to **E:\Microsoft Learning\2364\Labfiles\ Lab02a\Setup**. Double-click **Install.cmd** to set up the Virtual PC for this lab. Enter the Administrator's password when prompted, which is **Pa$$w0rd**.This command file sets up database security to allow the Student account to deploy to the SQL Server.

3. If you have already run through the lab or run one of the supplied solutions, you must run the CleanUpVB.cmd or CleanUpCS.cmd file located in the E:\Microsoft Learning\2364\ Labfiles\Lab02a folder. This script removes the managed code from SQL Server 2005 so that you can cleanly redeploy a new version.

4. In Visual Studio 2005, open the solution file for your preferred language. The Visual Basic solution is at E:\Microsoft Learning\2364\Labfiles\Lab02a\Solution\VB\NorthwindSQL\ NorthwindSql.sln. The Visual C# solution is at E:\Microsoft Learning\2364\Labfiles\Lab02a\ Solution\CS\NorthwindSQL\NorthwindSql.sln.

5. As Visual Studio 2005 loads the project, it displays the error message **Unable to connect to a database specified in the solution. Do you want to modify this database connection properties?** Click **Yes**.

6. If prompted to **Choose Data Source**, select **Microsoft SQL Server** and click **Continue**.

7. On the **Connection Properties** page, enter **london\sqlexpress** in the server name box, select **Use Windows Authentication**, and in the **Select or enter a database name** box, select **Northwind**.

8. Click **Test Connection**. If the test does not succeed then check the settings and correct if necessary. Click **OK** to complete the connection. Visual Studio finishes loading the project.

9. On the **Build** menu, click **Deploy Solution**.

10. Open Server Explorer. Expand the tree beneath Data Connections to locate the Tables folder. Right-click on the **Suppliers** table and then click **Open Table Definition**.

11. Scroll down the list of columns and add a new column called **WebService**. Set the Data Type for the column as **WebServiceType**. Save the table changes.

12. In Server Explorer, right-click on the **Suppliers** table and then click **Show Table Data**. In the data editor, enter suitable Uniform Resource Locators (URLs) in the WebService field, such as '**http://www.contoso.com/ProductService.asmx**' for the first supplier, and '**https://www.contoso.com/ProductService.asmx**' for the second supplier.

13. Open the Test Harness solution for your preferred language. The Visual Basic solution is at E:\Microsoft Learning\2364\Labfiles\Lab02a\Solution\VB\TestHarness\TestHarness.sln. The Visual C# solution is at E:\Microsoft Learning\2364\Labfiles\Lab02a\Solution\CS\TestHarness\ TestHarness.sln.

14. Run the Test Harness program and confirm that the first two suppliers have Web services available.

Exercise 1
Creating a Managed SQL Server 2005 Assembly

In this exercise, you will study the Technical Specification document that describes the details of the managed assembly that you must build. You will then create a SQL Server project and write the necessary code. This assembly will consist of a stored procedure, a user-defined function, and a UDT.

Scenario

Some suppliers now offer a Web Service for placing orders through the Internet. To store this additional information, you have decided to create a managed assembly for use within SQL Server 2005 that contains a UDT and some supporting code. The Suppliers table must be modified to include a new column based on the UDT.

Tasks	Supporting information
1. Open the Lab Toolkit and read the Program Design Specification for the NorthwindSQL component.	See the resource in the Lab Toolkit, *Northwind Traders Technical Specification: NorthWindSQL Class Library*.

2. Start Visual Studio 2005 and create a new project using the language of your choice. Name the project NorthwindSQL.	■ Create a project using the following settings:
	   • Template: **SQL Server Project**
	   • Name: **NorthwindSQL**

3. Add a database reference to the Northwind database.	■ If necessary, click **Yes** in the dialog box to enable SQL/CLR Debugging.
	■ Create a database reference using the following settings:
	   • Server Name: **london\sqlexpress**
	   • Security information: **Use Windows Authentication**
	   • Database: **Northwind**
	
	Tip If you have previously added a database reference to a project, you can select this reference from the list of existing database references.

4. Add an existing helper function to the project that contains RegEx code for validating Web URLs.	■ Add the following existing item to your project:
	   • **For Visual Basic**
	    E:\Microsoft Learning\2364\Labfiles\Lab02a\Start\VB\ HelperFunctions.vb
	   • **For Visual C#**
	    E:\Microsoft Learning\2364\Labfiles\Lab02a\Start\CS\ HelperFunctions.cs

(continued)

Tasks	Supporting information
5. Create a managed user-defined function.	See the resource in the Lab Toolkit, *Creating a User-Defined Function in Managed Code*. ■ Add a new user-defined function called **ValidateURLFormat**. ■ Modify the template code so that the **ValidateURLFormat** function returns a Boolean value and accepts a SqlString parameter. ■ Modify the existing template code within the method by returning the result of a call to the **ValidateURL** method on the **HelperFunctions** class. Pass the SqlString parameter to the **ValidateURL** method using the **ToString** method of the SqlString parameter.
6. Create managed stored procedure.	See the following resources in the Lab Toolkit: ■ *Creating stored procedures in Managed Code* ■ *Using the **Microsoft.SqlServer.Server** Namespace* ■ Add a new stored procedure to the project called **GetSecureSupplierWebServices**. ■ In the **GetSecureSupplierWebServices** function, declare local variables of the following type: • **SqlCommand** ■ Add code to create a new SqlCommand (System.Data.SqlClient.SqlCommand) variable. ■ Set the **CommandText** property of your SqlCommand variable to the following string: SELECT SupplierID, CompanyName, WebService.ToString() As WebService FROM Suppliers WHERE WebService IS NOT NULL AND WebService.Secure = 1 ■ Call the shared (static) **ExecuteAndSend** method of the SqlContext.Pipe property passing the command variable as the only method argument.
7. Create a managed UDT. This type splits a Web Service URL into three different parts: whether it uses secure communication, the Web site address, and the Web service file name.	See the resource in the Lab Toolkit, *Creating a User-Defined Type in Managed Code*. ■ Add a new UDT to the project, and name it **WebServiceType**. ■ Add Imports (Visual Basic)/using (Visual C#) statements for the **System.IO** namespace. ■ Within the **WebServiceType** struct, declare the following private variables in their indicated types: • is_Null (Boolean type) • m_WebService (string type) ■ Set the following arguments of the **SqlUserDefinedType** attribute: • Format argument equals Format.UserDefined • IsByteOrdered equals true • MaxByteSize equals 512 ■ Implement (inherit) IBinarySerialize.

(continued)

Tasks	Supporting information
7. *(continued)*	■ Create a **Read** method, which implements (overrides) the **IBinarySerialize.Read** method and accepts a **BinaryReader** as its only argument. ■ Assign the **WebService** property to the value of the **BinaryReader's ReadString** method. ■ Create a **Write** method, which implements (overrides) the **IBinarySerialize.Write** method and accepts a **BinaryWriter** as its only argument. ■ Use the **BinaryWriter's Write** method to assign its value to the **WebService** property. ■ Create public property accessors for the m_WebService variable, naming the property **WebService**. ■ Create read only public property accessors, naming the properties **WebSiteURL**, **ServiceFileName**, and **Secure**. • The **WebSiteURL** property retrieves the portion of the Web service name between http:// and the first "/" after the domain name. Consider creating a local string variable of the Web service URL value, remove the "http://" or "https://" from the string, and locate the position of the first occurrence of a "/" to determine the positions for the substring need. • The **ServiceFileName** property retrieves the portion of the Web service name after the first "/" following the domain name. Consider creating a local string variable of the Web service URL value, remove the "http://" or "https://" from the string, and locate the position of the first occurrence of a "/" to determine the positions for the substring need. • The **Secure** property evaluates the beginning of the Web service string, returning true if the Web service starts with "https://". Use one of the built-in string functions to check the beginning of the string variable to see whether it starts with "https://" or "http://". ■ Remove the existing code from within the **ToString** method and do the following: • Create an IF block and check the value of the is_Null variable. If true, return the string value **"NULL"**, else return the value of **m_WebService**. ■ Modify the existing code within the **IsNull** property to return the **is_Null** value. ■ Locate the **Null** property within the struct. After the creation of the WebServiceType variable, assign the **is_Null** field of the WebServiceType variable to **true** before the variable returns from the function call.

(continued)

Tasks	Supporting information
7. *(continued)*	■ Locate the **Parse** method within the struct. Replace the existing comment, "Put your code here," with the code described as follows: • Create an IF block that tests the result of a call to the **ValidateURL** method on the **HelperFunctions** class. Pass the SqlString parameter to the **ValidateURL** method using the **ToString** method of the SqlString parameter. • If the result of the **ValidateURL** function is **false**, throw an exception with an appropriate error message. • Create an instance of **WebServiceType** in a new variable and assign the m_WebService value of the new variable to a lower case String value of the SqlString parameter. ■ Remove the **Method1** method from the struct.
8. Build and deploy the project.	See the resource in the Lab Toolkit, *Debugging and Deploying Managed Code to SQL Server 2005*. ■ Build the project and correct any errors. Ignore any warnings about the use of inbuilt features that will be deprecated after the beta version of Visual Studio 2005. ■ Deploy the project to SQL Server 2005 using the **Build** menu.

Exercise 2
Debug the Managed Code

In this exercise, you will test and debug your managed code using Visual Studio .NET 2005. You will create a test script and use the integrated Structured Query Language (SQL) debugger to step through your managed code all within the same integrated development environment (IDE).

Scenario

To test your managed code, you must create a test script that tests the user-defined function, UDT, and stored procedure.

Tasks	Supporting information
1. Modify the Test.sql file to test the user-defined function.	■ Using Solution Explorer, expand the **TestScripts** folder. ■ Open the Test.sql file that Visual Studio .NET creates automatically when you add managed code to your project. ■ Modify the call to the **dbo.ValidateURLFormat** function, and pass a valid URL string such as **http://www.northwindtraders.com/ourservice.asmx** ■ Add a second call to the **dbo.ValidateURLFormat** function and pass an invalid URL string such as **http:///www.northwindtraders.com/ourservice.asmx** **Tip** When editing T-SQL scripts as you do in this exercise, the correct string delimiter is the single quotation mark symbol ('), not the double quotation mark symbol (").
2. Debug the ValidateURLFormat code.	See the resource in the Lab Toolkit, *Debugging and Deploying Managed Code to SQL Server 2005*. ■ Right-click **Test.sql** and then click **Debug Script**. ■ Use the regular debugging options to step through your managed code.
3. Add a column called **WebService** to the Suppliers table with a data type of **WebServiceType**.	■ Use Server Explorer to locate the **Suppliers** table within the **Northwind** database. ■ Right-click **Suppliers** and click **Open Table Definition**. ■ Add a new column to the table, and name it **WebService**. ■ Set the data type for the column as **dbo.WebServiceType**. ■ Save and close the table designer.

(*continued*)

Tasks	Supporting information
4. Test the managed UDT.	▪ Reopen the Test.sql file if it is closed. ▪ Modify the test script to include three **UPDATE** statements. Notice the subtle differences between these statements which are highlighted. In particular, notice the three "/. following .https:" in the third **SET** statement: • UPDATE Suppliers SET WebService = 'http://www.cohowinery.com/WebService.asmx' WHERE SupplierID = 1 • UPDATE Suppliers SET WebService = '**https**://www.**fourthcoffee**.com/WebService.asmx' WHERE SupplierID = 2 • UPDATE Suppliers SET WebService = '**https**:///www.**northwindtraders**.com/WebService.asmx' WHERE SupplierID = 3 ▪ Execute these statements without debugging. If you are notified that there were deployment errors, click **Yes** to continue. The error is simply a warning about the use of an inbuilt feature that will be deprecated after the beta version of Visual Studio 2005. The first two statements will succeed, but the third will fail because of the invalid URL format.
5. Test the managed stored procedure.	▪ Modify the test script to execute the **GetSecureSupplierWebServices** stored procedure. Also, remove or comment out the third UPDATE statement. You can comment out the statement by enclosing it in begin and end comment tags (/* ... */). ▪ Execute the statements without debugging. If you are notified that there were deployment errors, click **Yes** to continue. There may be warnings about the use of inbuilt features that will be deprecated after the beta version of Visual Studio 2005. ▪ View the **Output** tab at the bottom of the screen.
6. Close the project.	▪ Save and close the project.

Exercise 3
Working with Managed SQL

In this exercise, you will modify a console application that iterates through the results of a Transact-SQL statement that includes a **WebServiceType** column. ADO.NET code retrieves the data using a SqlDataReader, and the console windows displays the results. You will add the code to display the properties of the **WebServiceType** column.

Scenario

To test the functionality of your managed UDT, you have decided to create a simple test harness that displays the results of a Transact-SQL **SELECT** statement within a managed client application. This involves adding a reference to the managed assembly containing the UDT and working with it as you would any other managed type.

Tasks	Supporting information
1. Open the TestHarness solution.	■ Open the TestHarness project from the following location: • For Visual Basic E:\Microsoft Learning\2364\Labfiles\Lab02a\Start\VB\ TestHarness\TestHarness.sln • For Visual C# E:\Microsoft Learning\2364\Labfiles\Lab02a\Start\CS\ TestHarness\ TestHarness.sln
2. Add a reference to the **NorthwindSQL** assembly.	■ In the **Add Reference** dialog box, reference the **NorthwindSQL** assembly. The assembly is located in the following folder: My Documents\Visual Studio 2005\Projects\NorthwindSQL\ NorthwindSQL\bin\Debug\ for Visual C#, - or- My Documents\Visual Studio 2005\Projects\NorthwindSQL\ NorthwindSQL\bin\ for Visual Basic.
3. Modify the **GetSuppliers** function to display the WebServiceType information.	■ Locate the string variable **connString**, and change the data source to **london\sqlexpress**. ■ Locate the comment, "Your code goes here." ■ Create a WebServiceType variable. ■ Assign the **WebService** column from the SqlDataReader variable to the WebServiceType variable. ■ Use the **WriteLine** method of the **Console** class to display the following properties from the WebServiceType variable: • **Secure** • **WebSiteURL** • **ServiceFileName**

(continued)

Tasks	Supporting information
4. Test the application.	▪ Build the solution. Ignore any warnings about the use of inbuilt features that will be deprecated after the beta version of Visual Studio 2005. ▪ Start the TestHarness application without debugging and confirm that the first two suppliers have Web services available.
5. Close the project.	▪ Close and save the project.

Lab 2B: Working with XML in Visual Studio 2005 and SQL Server 2005

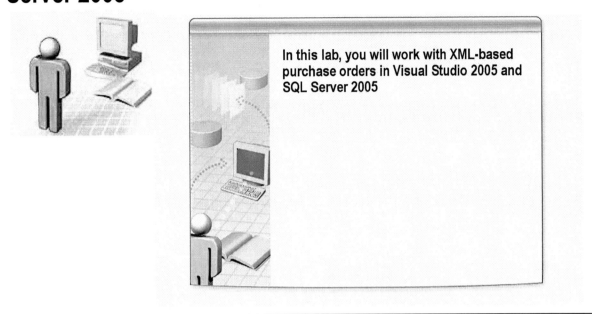

In this lab, you will work with XML-based purchase orders in Visual Studio 2005 and SQL Server 2005

After completing this lab, you will be able to:

- Create XML columns in SQL Server databases.
- Add XML data to XML columns.
- Create XML schemas.
- Publish XML schemas so that they can be accessed both programmatically and manually.
- Validate XML documents using schemas.
- Process and query XML data using .NET classes.

Lab Toolkit Resources

If necessary, use one or more of the following Lab Toolkit resources to help you complete this lab:

- Northwind Traders Technical Specification: NorthwindXML Class Library
- Northwind Traders Technical Specification: Purchase Order Data Access Application
- XML Schema Designer Overview
- Using the **System.Xml** Namespace

Estimated time to complete this lab: 75 minutes

Lab Setup

For this lab, you will use the LONDON Virtual PC.

To prepare for this lab:

1. Start the LONDON Virtual PC if it is not already started. You can either continue working with the LONDON Virtual PC if you have already completed Lab 2A, or you can complete this lab on its own, as there are no dependency issues between Lab 2A and this lab. However, do not use the LONDON UNIT 1 Virtual PC that you used in Unit 1.

2. Log on as **Student** with a password of **Pa$$w0rd**.

3. Click the **Labfiles** Toolbar at the bottom right of the screen and navigate to **Lab02b\Setup**.

4. Click **Install** to setup the Virtual PC for this lab. This command file sets up database security to allow the Student account to modify the structure of the Northwind database.

5. Enter the Administrators password when prompted, which is **Pa$$w0rd**.

6. Press any key to exit the setup command procedure.

 Caution The setup procedure for this lab performs operations with SQL Server. If you have recently started the virtual PC, the database server may not have completed its startup. If you run the install script and you see any of the following errors, wait a few minutes and then try to run the install script again:

- Client unable to establish connection.
- Shared Memory Provider: The system cannot find the file specified.
- Timeout expired.

Lab Solution Files

There are Visual Basic and Visual C# starter and solution files associated with the labs in this workshop. The starter files are located in the E:\Microsoft Learning\2364\Labfiles\Lab02b\Start folder, and the solution files are located in E:\Microsoft Learning\2364\Labfiles\Lab02b\Solution folder, both on the Virtual PC.

Follow the following steps to run one of the supplied solutions:

1. Log on as **Student** with a password of **Pa$$w0rd**.

2. Start Windows Explorer, and navigate to **E:\Microsoft Learning\2364\Labfiles\Lab02b\ Solution\..** Double-click **InstallSolution.cmd** to set up the Virtual PC for these solution files. This command file sets up database security to allow the Student account to deploy to the SQL Server, installs a schema in Internet Information Services (IIS), and sets up some other test files.

3. Enter the Administrators password when prompted, which is **Pa$$w0rd**.

4. Press any key to exit the setup command procedure.

5. In Visual Studio 2005, open the solution file for your preferred language. The Visual Basic solution is at E:\Microsoft Learning\2364\Labfiles\Lab02b\Solution\VB\NorthwindXML\ NorthwindXML.sln. The Visual C# solution is at E:\Microsoft Learning\2364\Labfiles\ Lab02b\Solution\CS\NorthwindXML\NorthwindXML.sln.

6. As Visual Studio 2005 loads the project, it displays the error message **Unable to connect to a Database specified in the solution. Do you want to modify this Database connection properties?** Click **Yes**.

7. If prompted to **Choose Data Source**, select **Microsoft SQL Server** and click **Continue**.

8. On the Connection Properties page, type **london\sqlexpress** in the server name box, select **Use Windows Authentication**, and, in the **Select or enter a database name** box, select **Northwind**.

9. Click **Test Connection**. If the test does not succeed, then check the settings and correct if necessary. Click **OK** to complete the connection. Visual Studio finishes loading the project.

10. On the **Build** menu, click **Deploy Solution**.

11. Open the Test Harness solution for your preferred language. The Visual Basic solution is at E:\Microsoft Learning\2364\Labfiles\Lab02b\Solution\VB\TestHarnessXml\ TestHarnessXml.sln. The Visual C# solution is at E:\Microsoft Learning\2364\Labfiles\Lab02b\ Solution\CS\ TestHarnessXml\TestHarnessXml.sln.

12. Run the Test Harness program and verify that you are notified that the purchase order has been added.

Exercise 1
Creating a SQL Server Project for Handling XML Data

In this exercise, you will create a new SQL Server project. Using the development tools in the project, you will create a new table for storing purchase orders that will eventually be sent to suppliers. You will also create a new stored procedure in managed code for adding Purchase Order documents to the table.

Scenario

The company has decided that it will reorder products from its suppliers through an automated procurement application. The application will send XML-based purchase orders over the Internet to the suppliers. The Northwind database must be modified so that it can store the XML-based purchase orders before they are sent to the suppliers. All purchase-order documents must be added to the database using a stored procedure. You will therefore create a new table that includes a column with the XML data type. You will then create the stored procedure for adding purchase orders to the table.

Tasks	Supporting information
1. Open the Resource Toolkit and read the Program Design Specification for the **NorthwindXML** component.	See the resource in the Lab Toolkit, *Northwind Traders Technical Specification: NorthwindXML Class Library*.
2. Start Visual Studio 2005 and create a new SQL Server project using either Visual C# or Visual Basic. Name the project **NorthwindXML**.	▪ Create a project using the following settings: 　• Template: **SQL Server Project** 　• Name: **NorthwindXML**
3. Add a database connection to the **Northwind** database.	▪ If necessary, click **Yes** in the dialog box to enable SQL/CLR Debugging. ▪ In the **Connection Properties** dialog box that appears, type **london\sqlexpress** in the **Select or enter a server name** drop-down list. ▪ Ensure that the **Use Windows Authentication** option is selected. ▪ From the **Select or enter a database name** drop-down list, select **Northwind**. ▪ Click **OK**. 　**Tip** If you have previously added a database reference to another project, you can select this reference from the list of existing database references.

(continued)

Tasks	Supporting information
4. Create the **SupplierPO** table.	▪ Open Server Explorer. ▪ Expand the **london\sqlexpress.Northwind.dbo** data connection. ▪ Right-click **Tables** and then click **Add New Table**. ▪ Add a column and name it **PO_ID**, with a data type of int. ▪ Add a column and name it **SupplierID**, with a data type of int. ▪ Add a column and name it **PurchaseOrderXML**, with a data type of xml. ▪ Clear the **Allow Nulls** check boxes for all three columns that you have just created. ▪ Right-click the **PO_ID** column and then click **Set Primary Key**. ▪ From the **View** menu, click **Properties Window**. ▪ In the Properties window, select PO_ID as the **Identity Column**. ▪ Change the **Name** property to **SupplierPO**. ▪ From the **File** menu, click **Save All**.

5. Create the **AddPO** stored procedure.	▪ From the **Project** menu, click **Add Stored Procedure**.
	▪ Name the new stored procedure **AddPO**.
	▪ Modify the AddPO procedure definition so that it accepts two string parameters named **POXml** and **SupplierID**.
	▪ In place of the comment, "**Put your code here**", write your own code in the manner specified below:
	  • Start a **try** block, declare a SqlCommand variable, and name the variable **.command**.
	  • Add Imports (Visual Basic)/using (Visual C#) statements for the **System.Data.SqlClient** namespace.
	  • Create a variable of type System.Data.SqlClient.SqlCommand and set it to a new instance of that type.
	  • Set the **CommandText** property of the **command** object to the following string:
	
	`"INSERT SupplierPO (SupplierID, PurchaseOrderXML) VALUES (" + SupplierID + ", '" + POXml + "')"`
	
	  • Call the shared (static) **ExecuteAndSend** method of the **SqlContext.Pipe** property, passing the command object as the only argument.
	  • End the **try** block.
	  • Add a **catch** block that catches an **Exception** object.
	  • In the **catch** block, throw a new exception with a message of **The purchase order could not be added to the database**.

(continued)

Tasks	Supporting information
5. *(continued)*	■ From the **File** menu, click **Save All**. ■ From the **Build** menu, click **Build NorthwindXML**. Ignore any warnings about unused variables. ■ Resolve any build errors if they occur. Then from the **Build** menu, click **Deploy NorthwindXML**. ■ Leave Visual Studio running. You will use it in the next exercise.

Exercise 2
Creating an XML Schema for Purchase Orders

In this exercise, you will create an XML schema that can be used to validate the data in a purchase order document before it is added to the database.

Scenario

The company wants to validate the XML-based documents that represent purchase orders before they are added to the database. Although XML documents can be automatically validated for correct syntax (known as *well-formedness*), the actual contents of the XML usually need validating as well. One way to validate XML content is to use an XML schema that defines the elements and attributes (and other content) that an XML document must contain. You will use the new XML schema designer in Visual Studio to create the appropriate schema. This tool allows you to drag and drop columns from a database to your schema to make schema creation an easy and quick task.

Tasks	Supporting information
1. Create an XML Schema.	If you are working with Visual C#, do the following: ■ From the **File** menu, point to **New** and then click **File**. ■ Select **XML Schema** from the list of available templates, and then click **Open**. If you are working with Visual Basic, do the following: ■ From the **Project** menu, click **Add Existing Item**. ■ Navigate to the **E:\Microsoft Learning\2364\Labfiles\Lab02b\Start** folder. ■ Select **POSchema.xsd**. ■ Click **Add**. ■ In the Solution Explorer window, double-click the file you have just added.
2. Open the Resource Toolkit and read the XML Schema Designer Overview.	See the resource in the Lab Toolkit, *XML Schema Designer Overview*.

(continued)

Tasks	Supporting information
3. Add elements to the schema.	■ In the Server Explorer window, expand your database connection and navigate to the **Suppliers** table.
	■ Select the following columns:
	• **SupplierID**
	• **CompanyName**
	• **Address**
	• **City**
	• **Region**
	• **PostalCode**
	■ Drag the selected columns to the schema designer surface.
	■ In the Server Explorer window, expand the **Supplier Orders** table.
	■ Select the **OrderDate** and **RequiredDate** columns.
	■ Drag the selected columns to the **Suppliers** element table on the schema designer surface.
	■ In the Server Explorer window, expand the **Supplier Order Details** table.
	■ Select the **ProductID** and the **UnitsOnOrder** columns.
	■ Drag the selected columns to the **Supplier Orders** element table on the schema designer surface.
	■ If you are working with Visual C#, from the **File** menu, click **Save XMLSchema1.xsd As**.
	■ If you are working with Visual Basic, from the **File** menu, click **Save POSchema.xsd As**.
	■ In the **Save File As** dialog box, navigate to the root of the **C:** drive.
	■ Click the **Create New Folder** button, enter a new folder name, **NWindSchemas**, and then click **OK**.
	■ Enter **POSchema** in the **File name** text box, and select **XML Schema Files** from the **Save as type** drop-down list. Then click **Save**.
	■ Close Visual Studio.

Exercise 3
Publishing XML Schemas

In this exercise, you will create a virtual directory for publishing the Purchase Order schema.

Scenario

The company wants to publish the XML schema you created in Exercise 2 so that it can be easily accessed by applications in the enterprise as well as potentially by external organizations such as suppliers. You will use Internet Information Services (IIS) to create the virtual directory so that the schema can be accessed programmatically or manually using Hypertext Transfer Protocol (HTTP).

Tasks	Supporting information
1. Create a schema virtual directory.	■ From the **Start** menu, click **Control Panel**. ■ If necessary, click **Switch to Classic View** and then double-click **Administrative Tools**. ■ Right-click **Internet Information Services**, and then click **Run as**. ■ Select **The following user** option. ■ Ensure **Administrator** is entered in the **User name** textbox, and type **Pa$$w0rd** in the **Password** box. ■ Click **OK**. ■ In the Internet Information Services console, expand the **LONDON (local computer)** node and then expand the **Web Sites** node. ■ Right-click **Default Web Site**, point to **New**, and then click **Virtual Directory**. ■ In the Virtual Directory Creation Wizard, click **Next**. ■ In the **Alias** box, type **NorthwindSchemas**, and then click **Next**. ■ Click **Browse**, and then navigate to the **C:\NWindSchemas** folder. ■ Click **OK** and then click **Next**. ■ Click **Next**, and then click **Finish**. ■ Close **Internet Information Services** and **Control Panel**.

Exercise 4
Validating and Processing XML Documents

In this exercise, you will create a test application that emulates a data access layer component. The application will read purchase-order XML files. It will then use the schema you created in Exercise 2 (and published in Exercise 3) to validate the contents of the purchase orders. If the purchase-order XML files are both valid and well formed, the application will query the contents to determine the supplier to whom these purchase-order XML files should be sent. The application will then submit the XML contents to SQL Server for storing in the database table that you created in Exercise 1. If they are invalid, the application will report the errors that it has found.

Scenario

The company wants to create a data-access component for reading XML-based purchase orders and validating them against the schema you developed in Exercise 2. The component should then submit valid purchase orders to the managed stored procedure you created in Exercise 1. You have decided to design and develop a test application that performs these functions to help you learn how to load, validate, and process XML documents that will be submitted to SQL Server for storage.

Tasks	Supporting information
1. Open the Resource Toolkit and read the Technical Specification for the Purchase Order Data Access Application and the Using the System.Xml Namespace resource.	See the following resources in the Lab Toolkit: ■ *Northwind Traders Technical Specification - Purchase Order Data Access Application* ■ *Using the System.Xml Namespace*
2. Start Visual Studio 2005 and create a console project using either Visual C# or Visual Basic. Name the project **TestHarnessXML**.	■ Create a project using the following settings: • Template: **Console Application** • Name: **TestHarnessXML**
3. Add purchase order XML files.	■ Using Windows Explorer, create a folder in the root of the C drive and name it **TestXML**. ■ Copy the GoodPO.xml and BadPO.xml files from the E:\Microsoft Learning\2364\Labfiles\Lab02b\Start folder to the C:\TestXML folder.
4. Add a starter file.	■ If you are working with Visual C#, in the Solution Explorer window, right-click **Program.cs**, and then click **Delete**. Click **OK**. ■ If you are working with Visual Basic, in the Solution Explorer window, right-click **Module1.vb**, and then click **Delete**. Click **OK**. ■ From the **Project** menu, click **Add Existing Item**. ■ If you are working with *C#*, browse to the **E:\Microsoft Learning\2364\Labfiles\Lab02b\Start\CS** folder and then select **Program.cs**. ■ If you are working with Visual Basic, browse to the **E:\Microsoft Learning\2364\Labfiles\Lab02b\Start\VB** folder and then select **Module1.vb**. ■ Click **Add** to add the selected file to your project.

(continued)

Tasks	Supporting information
5. Complete the **AddPurchaseOrder** function.	■ In the Solution Explorer window, right-click the file you have just added and then click **Open**. ■ Replace the **Your Code goes here** comment with code as described in the following steps.
6. Create an **XmlDocument** object and load purchase order XML from a file.	■ Declare an XmlDocument variable named **xDoc** and set it to a new instance of the **XmlDocument** class. ■ Call the **Load** method of the **xDoc** object, and pass in a string that contains the path to **C:\TestXML\GoodPO.xml**. ■ Declare a string variable called **poXML** and set it to the **OuterXml** property of the **xDoc** object.
7. Create an **XmlNamespaceManager** object to manage the namespaces to be used for the **XmlDocument** object you have just created.	■ Declare an XmlNamespaceManager variable named **nsManager** and set it to a new instance of the **XmlNamespaceManager** class, passing in the **NameTable** property of the **xDoc** object as a parameter. ■ Call the **AddNamespace** method of the **nsManager** object, passing in "**XMLSchema.xsd**" as the prefix parameter, and "http://tempuri.org/XMLSchema.xsd" as the url parameter.
8. Create **XmlNode** objects that will hold the SupplierID for the purchase order. Then use an **XPath** query to extract the SupplierID. Store the SupplierID in a string variable.	■ Declare an XmlNode variable and name it **xNode**, and a string variable named **supplierID**. ■ Declare an XmlNode variable named **xRoot**, and set it to the **DocumentElement** property of the **xDoc** object. ■ Set the xNode variable to the result of calling the **SelectSingleNode** method of the **xRoot** object. Pass in "//XMLSchema.xsd:SupplierID" as the xpath parameter and **nsManager** as the nsmgr parameter. ■ Set the supplierID variable to the **Value** property of the **FirstChild** property of the **xNode** object.
9. Create an **XmlSchemaSet** object. Add the schema you created and published earlier in this lab to the **XmlSchemaSet** object.	■ Declare an XmlSchemaSet variable and name it **schemaSet**, and then set it to a new instance of the **XmlSchemaSet** class. ■ If you are working with Visual C#, call the **Add** method of the **schemaSet** object, passing in **null** as the targetNamespace parameter, and "**http://localhost/NorthwindSchemas/POSchema.xsd**" as the url parameter. ■ If you are working with Visual Basic, call the **Add** method of the **schemaSet** object, passing in **Nothing** as the targetNamespace parameter, and "**http://localhost/NorthwindSchemas/ POSchema.xsd**" as the url parameter.

(continued)

Tasks	Supporting information
10. Create an **XmlTextReader** object for reading the purchase order XML.	▪ If you are working with Visual C#, declare an XmlTextReader variable and name it **xReader**, and then set it to a new instance of the **XmlTextReader** class. Pass in the poXML variable as the xmlFragment parameter, **XmlNodeType.Document** as the fragType parameter, and **null** as the context parameter. ▪ If you are working with Visual Basic, declare an XmlTextReader variable and name it **xReader**, and set it to a new instance of the **XmlTextReader** class. Pass in the poXML variable as the xmlFragment parameter, **XmlNodeType.Document** as the fragType parameter, and **Nothing** as the context parameter.
11. Create an **XmlReaderSettings** object to control how the purchase order XML will be validated.	▪ Declare an XmlReaderSettings variable and name it **settings**, and set it to a new instance of the **XmlReaderSettings** class. ▪ Set the **ValidationType** property of the **settings** object to **ValidationType.Schema**. ▪ Set the **ValidationFlags** property of the **settings** object to **XmlSchemaValidationFlags.ReportValidationWarnings**. ▪ Set the **Schemas** property of the **settings** object to the **schemaSet** object. ▪ Set the **ValidationEventHandler** property of the **settings** object to a new instance of the **ValidationEventHandler** class, passing in ValidationCallBack as the only parameter. (Hint: Review the solution files for an example of how to manage this **ValidationEventHandler** property if you are not familiar with adding callback event handlers.)
12. Create an **XmlReader** object that performs validation of the XML in the **XmlTextReader** object, using the validation settings contained in the **XmlReaderSettings** object.	▪ Declare an XmlReader variable and name it **reader**, and then set it to the result of calling the **Create** method of the intrinsic **XmlReader** object. Pass in **xReader** as the reader parameter, and **settings** as the settings parameter. ▪ Call the **Write** method of the **Console** object, passing in "Processing Purchase Order" as the only parameter. ▪ Construct a loop that writes a single period to the **Console** object while **reader.Read()** remains true. ▪ After the loop you have just created, determine whether the errText variable is equal to the empty string… If it is *not* equal to the empty string, throw a new Exception with a message of the errText variable.

(continued)

Tasks	Supporting information
13. Connect to SQL Server to execute the **AddPO** stored procedure in the Northwind database. Pass in the SupplierID and the purchase order XML strings as parameters to the stored procedure.	■ After your block for determining whether errText is equal to the empty string, declare a SqlParameter variable called **paramPO**, and set it to a new instance of the **SqlParameter** class. Pass in "**POXml**" as the parameterName parameter, and **SqlDbType.VarChar** as the dbType parameter.
	■ Declare a SqlParameter variable, and name it **paramSupplierID**, and then set it to a new instance of the **SqlParameter** class. Pass in "**SupplierID**" as the parameterName parameter, and **SqlDbType.VarChar** as the dbType parameter.
	■ Declare a string variable and name it **connString**, and then set it to **data source=london\sqlexpress;initial catalog=northwind;integrated security=true**.
	■ Declare a SqlConnection variable and name it **conn**, and set it to a new instance of the **SqlConnection** class. Pass in **connString** as the only parameter.
	■ Declare a **SqlCommand** variable and name it **cmd**, and set it to a new instance of the **SqlCommand** class.
	■ Set the **Connection** property of the **cmd** object to the **conn** object.
	■ Set the **CommandType** property of the **cmd** object to **CommandType.StoredProcedure**.
	■ Set the **CommandText** property of the **cmd** object to **.AddPO**.
	■ Set the **Value** property of **paramPO** to **poXML**.
	■ Set the **Value** property of **paramSupplierID** to **supplierID**.
	■ Call the **Add** method of the **Parameters** property of the **cmd** object. Pass in paramPO as the only parameter.
	■ Call the **Add** method of the **Parameters** property of the **cmd** object. Pass in paramSupplierID as the only parameter.
	■ Call the **Open** method of the **conn** object.
	■ Call the **ExecuteNonQuery** method of the **cmd** object.
	■ Call the **Close** method of the **conn** object.
14. Provide feedback to the user.	■ Call the **WriteLine** method of the **Console** object, without passing in any parameters.
	■ Call the **WriteLine** method of the **Console** object, passing in "Purchase Order Added. Press any key to exit..." as the only parameter.
15. Save the project.	■ From the **File** menu, click **Save All**.

(continued)

Tasks	Supporting information

16. Test the solution with a valid purchase order.	■ From the **Build** menu, click **Build TestHarnessXML**.
	
	■ Resolve any build errors if they occur.
	
	■ Run the application without debugging.
	
	■ When you are notified that the purchase order has been added, press ENTER to exit the console application.
	
	In the Server Explorer window, expand the following nodes:
	
	   • **Data Connections**
	
	   • **London\sqlexpress.Northwind.dbo**
	
	   • **Tables**
	
	■ Right-click **SupplierPO** and click **Show Table Data**. Verify that a row has been added that contains XML representing a purchase order.

17. Test the solution with an invalid purchase order.	■ Modify your code near the top of the **AddPurchaseOrder** function so that it loads the BadPO.xml file instead of the GoodPO.xml file. ■ From the **Build** menu, click **Build TestHarnessXML**. ■ Resolve any build errors if they occur, then run the application without debugging. ■ Read the error message in the console. The BadPO.xml file is well formed, but the **CompanyName** element has not been spelled correctly, so it does not pass the validation test of the schema. ■ Press ENTER to exit the console application. ■ Close Visual Studio. You have now completed this lab.

Lab Discussion

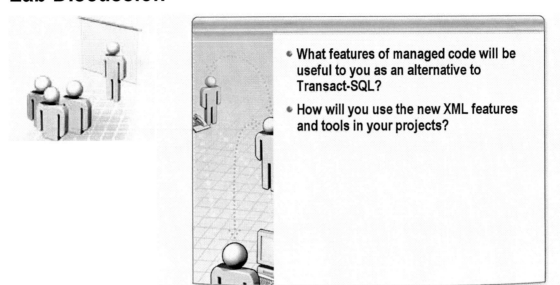

- What features of managed code will be useful to you as an alternative to Transact-SQL?
- How will you use the new XML features and tools in your projects?

In this lab, you have learned how to create managed code for use within SQL Server 2005.

Discuss with the class the advantages that managed code has over Transact-SQL. Also discuss how XML eases a lot of development and infrastructure problems.

Best Practices

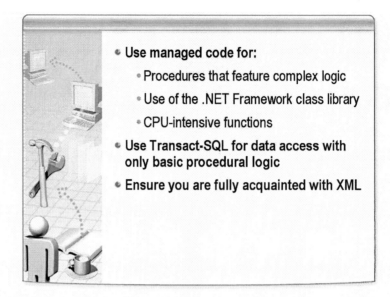

- **Use managed code for:**
  - Procedures that feature complex logic
  - Use of the .NET Framework class library
  - CPU-intensive functions
- **Use Transact-SQL for data access with only basic procedural logic**
- **Ensure you are fully acquainted with XML**

Managed Code

You should use managed code for creating database objects in the following situations:

- You require complex programmatic logic to complete a task.
  The managed .NET Framework languages provide powerful features such as object orientation, structured exception handling, and advanced conditional constructs. Features such as namespaces and the ability to create private helper functions make complex logic more manageable.

- You need to utilize the .NET Framework base class library.
  The base class library contains powerful classes that can perform tasks such as encryption, the calling of Web services, working with the file system, and many other tasks that are difficult or impossible with Transact-SQL.

- Your required functionality will be CPU-intensive.
  Because of the compiled nature of managed code, any functionality that is CPU intensive will run more efficiently than it would if implemented using Transact-SQL.

Transact-SQL

You should use Transact-SQL for creating database objects when the code will mainly perform data access with little or no procedural logic. This is because Transact-SQL is optimized for set-based operations on data. You should avoid creating managed database objects whose sole purpose is to work with traditional database objects such as tables and views; in this case, use Transact-SQL instead.

XML

You should ensure that you are fully acquainted with how to manipulate, validate, and store XML in Visual Studio 2005 and SQL Server 2005. XML has been rapidly accepted as the standard format for data interchange and manipulation over the Internet, and it is becoming ever more widely used in enterprise-level applications.

Unit 3: Building Data Components in Visual Studio 2005

Contents

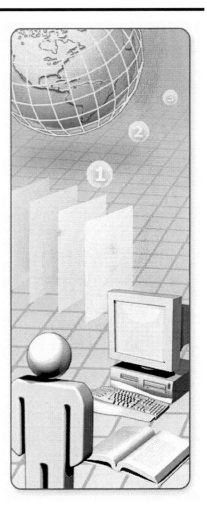

Information in this document, including URL and other Internet Web site references, is subject to change without notice. Unless otherwise noted, the example companies, organizations, products, domain names, e-mail addresses, logos, people, places, and events depicted herein are fictitious, and no association with any real company, organization, product, domain name, e-mail address, logo, person, place or event is intended or should be inferred. Complying with all applicable copyright laws is the responsibility of the user. Without limiting the rights under copyright, no part of this document may be reproduced, stored in or introduced into a retrieval system, or transmitted in any form or by any means (electronic, mechanical, photocopying, recording, or otherwise), or for any purpose, without the express written permission of Microsoft Corporation.

The names of manufacturers, products, or URLs are provided for informational purposes only and Microsoft makes no representations and warranties, either expressed, implied, or statutory, regarding these manufacturers or the use of the products with any Microsoft technologies. The inclusion of a manufacturer or product does not imply endorsement of Microsoft of the manufacturer or product. Links are provided to third party sites. Such sites are not under the control of Microsoft and Microsoft is not responsible for the contents of any linked site or any link contained in a linked site, or any changes or updates to such sites. Microsoft is not responsible for webcasting or any other form of transmission received from any linked site. Microsoft is providing these links to you only as a convenience, and the inclusion of any link does not imply endorsement of Microsoft of the site or the products contained therein.

Microsoft may have patents, patent applications, trademarks, copyrights, or other intellectual property rights covering subject matter in this document. Except as expressly provided in any written license agreement from Microsoft, the furnishing of this document does not give you any license to these patents, trademarks, copyrights, or other intellectual property.

© 2005 Microsoft Corporation. All rights reserved.

Microsoft, ActiveX, IntelliSense, MSDN, MS-DOS, PowerPoint, Visual Basic, Visual C#, Visual SourceSafe, Visual Studio, Visual Web Developer, Windows, Windows Media, Windows NT, and Windows Server are either registered trademarks or trademarks of Microsoft Corporation in the United States and/or other countries.

The names of actual companies and products mentioned herein may be the trademarks of their respective owners.

Overview

- New Features of ADO.NET 2.0
- Demonstration: Asynchronous Processing In ADO.NET
- Visual Studio 2005 Wizards and Designers
- Demonstration: Creating Data Components
- Lab 3: Accessing Data Using ADO.NET
- Lab Discussion

Every developer writes code to access data, and in a typical three-tier application, writing data access components forms a significant part of the development effort. This unit introduces the enhancements to ADO.NET (ActiveX® Data Object) 2.0 and the new data wizards available in Microsoft® Visual Studio® 2005.

Objectives

After completing this unit, you will be able to:

- Write data provider-agnostic ADO.NET code.

- Create data components using Visual Studio 2005.

- Use the enhanced features of typed DataSets in Visual Studio 2005.

New Features of ADO.NET 2.0

- **Multiple active result sets**
  - One connection can host more than one result set
  - Reduces number of connections on a database
- **Asynchronous operations**
  - Begin a data access operation, continue with other tasks, and then later end the original operation
- **Batch updates**
  - Update multiple rows in one batch
  - Use the UpdateBatchSize property of the DataAdapter

The .NET Framework 2.0 provides two key ways to access data: ADO.NET 2.0 and **System.Xml**. ADO.NET 2.0 encompasses the classes in the **System.Data** namespace and is recommended for accessing data from a variety of relational data sources. **System.Xml** includes new features to simplify and extend the data access methods that you can use when working with XML data in your applications.

ADO.NET 2.0 provides a number of key enhancements over previous versions of ADO.NET, including multiple active result sets (MARS), asynchronous operations, and batch updates.

Multiple Active Result Sets (MARS)

In previous releases of ADO.NET, you could have only one result set open within one connection at a time. This meant that you had to close a **SqlDataReader** or a **DataSet** before reusing the connection. MARS enables you to use one database connection to host multiple result sets simultaneously, so you can execute asynchronous commands using the same connection. By default, MARS is enabled on connections to MARS-enabled hosts, such as Microsoft SQL Server™ 2005.

Asynchronous operations

ADO.NET 1.1 and earlier required your data access operations to be synchronous. ADO.NET 2.0 includes new methods for the **Connection** and **Command** classes that enable you to execute asynchronous operations. You can begin a data access operation, continue with other application tasks, and then call the end method at a later time to complete the operation. If required, you can use callback functions to end the operation when it is complete.

Batch updates

ADO.NET 2.0 enables you to execute multiple **DataSet** updates in one batch. In previous versions, each row modification in the **DataSet** resulted in a separate update operation against the database, sometimes impeding performance. Setting the **UpdateBatchSize** property of the relevant **DataAdapter** object enables you to configure the number of rows to be included in each batch.

Demonstration: Asynchronous Processing in ADO.NET

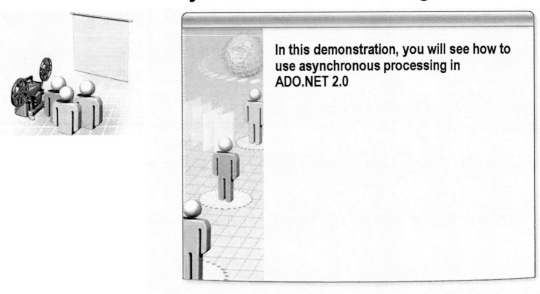

In this demonstration, you will see how to use asynchronous processing in ADO.NET 2.0. The instructor will:

1. Review code that performs asynchronous operations.

2. Run an application that performs asynchronous operations.

Visual Studio 2005 Wizards and Designers

- Data Source Configuration Wizard
- TableAdapter Configuration Wizard
- TableAdapter Query Configuration Wizard
- Preview Data Dialog Box

Visual Studio 2005 also includes a number of new wizards and designers to help you create and manage ADO.NET data components in your applications. These include:

- *Data Source Configuration Wizard* - You can use this wizard to create and edit data sources in your projects from databases, Web services, objects, and local data files.

- *TableAdapter Configuration Wizard* - You can use this wizard to create and edit strongly typed data components based on Transact-SQL statements, new stored procedures, and existing stored procedures.

- *TableAdapter Query Configuration Wizard* - You can use this wizard to create and edit the details of a query component that you can then execute by calling a method of the component's **TableAdapter** object.

- *Preview Data Dialog Box* - You can use this dialog box to preview data returned by the **TableAdapter** queries in a project.

These wizards, in addition to the new functionality of ADO.NET 2.0, result in a powerful system for accessing relational data and working with typed **DataSets**.

Demonstration: Creating Data Components

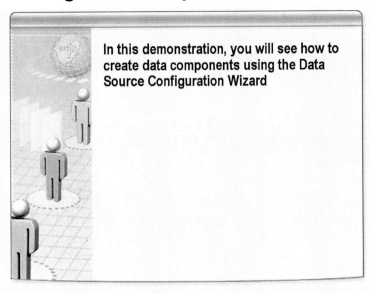

In this demonstration, you will see how to create data components using the Data Source Configuration Wizard

In this demonstration, you will see how to create data components using the Data Source Configuration Wizard. The instructor will:

1. Create a class library project.

2. Create a data source using data returned from an existing stored procedure in a SQL Server database.

3. Create a test project.

4. Write code to pass parameters to the stored procedure.

5. Write code to display the returned data in a **DataGridView** control.

6. Review the wizard-generated code.

Lab 3: Accessing Data Using ADO.NET

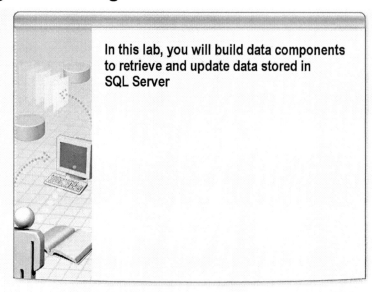

In this lab, you will build data components to retrieve and update data stored in SQL Server

After completing this lab, you will be able to:

- Create data components using Visual Studio 2005.

- Use the enhanced features of typed **DataSets** in Visual Studio 2005.

- Write data provider agnostic ADO.NET code.

 Important You can choose to program with either Microsoft Visual C#® or Microsoft Visual Basic® in this workshop. Code samples and lab solutions are provided in both programming languages. If you prefer, you can choose to perform some labs using one programming language, and perform others using the other language. However, once you start a lab, you should complete all the lab exercises using the same programming language.

Lab Setup

For this lab, you will use the LONDON Virtual PC.

To prepare for this lab:

1. If LONDON Virtual PC is still running after the previous lab, on the **Action** menu, click **Close**. The **Action** menu is visible when the Virtual PC is running in windowed mode, but not when it is running full-screen. If you are running the Virtual PC full-screen, press <RIGHT>ALT+ENTER to switch to windowed mode.

2. In the **Close** window, select **Turn off and delete changes** and then click **OK**.

3. Start the LONDON Virtual PC if it is not already started. Do not use the LONDON UNIT 1 Virtual PC for this lab.

4. Log on as **Student** with a password **Pa$$w0rd**.

5. Click the **Labfiles** toolbar at the bottom right of the screen and navigate to **Lab03\Setup**.

6. Click **Install** to set up the Virtual PC for this lab.

7. Enter the Administrator's password when prompted, which is **Pa$$w0rd**.

8. Press any key to exit the setup command procedure.

 Caution The setup procedure for this lab performs operations with SQL Server. If you have recently started the virtual PC, the database server may not have completed its startup. If you run the install script and you see any of the following errors, wait a few minutes and then try to run the install script again:

- Client unable to establish connection.
- Shared Memory Provider: The system cannot find the file specified.
- Timeout expired.

Lab Toolkit Resources

Use the following Lab Toolkit resources to help you complete this lab:

- Northwind Traders Technical Specification: Customer and Customer Order Details Maintenance Components
- Data Source Wizards Overview
- Adding a Data Source to a Project
- Configuring a Data Component to Use Existing Stored Procedures
- Using a DataGridView with a Data Source Component
- Adding a Data Component to an Existing Data Source
- Adding a Query to a Data Source
- Using a Data Source Query

Estimated time to complete this lab: **90 minutes**

Lab Solution Files

There are Visual Basic and Visual C# solution files associated with the labs in this workshop. The lab solution files are located in the folder E:\Microsoft Learning\2364\Labfiles\Lab03\Solution on the Virtual PCs.

 Important If you want to run either of the supplied solutions, you must first execute a setup script to ensure that the stored procedures used by this program exist in the Northwind database in SQL Server.

To execute the command procedure, start Windows Explorer and navigate to **E:\Microsoft Learning\2364\Labfiles\Lab03\Solution**. Double-click **InstallSolution.bat** to set up the stored procedures.

Exercise 1
Creating a Data Component

In this exercise, you will study the Technical Specification document that describes the details of the component that you must build. You will then use the Data Source Configuration Wizard to build the **ListOrdersTableAdapter** component, a class that returns a list of orders to the calling application using existing stored procedures in the Northwind database. This component will consist of a typed **DataSet** exposing the functionality to view, insert, update, and delete orders in the Northwind database.

Scenario

Employees require an application that will allow them to view and update customer orders. You need to create a component that can be used to display and update orders using existing stored procedures in the Northwind database. You also need to create a Microsoft Windows® application test harness to debug and test the component.

Tasks	Supporting information
1. Open the **Lab Toolkit** and read the Program Design Specification for the **ListOrders** component.	In the Lab Toolkit, see the following resources: ■ *Northwind Traders Technical Specification: Customer and Customer Order Details Maintenance Components* ■ *Data Source Wizards Overview* ■ Read the Data Source Wizards Overview Lab Toolkit resource to understand how to use the wizards to perform the exercises in this lab.
2. Start Visual Studio 2005 and create a new project using the language of your choice. Name the project **NorthwindComponent**.	■ Create a project using the following settings: • Template: **Class Library** • Name: **NorthwindComponent** ■ Delete Class1.
3. Add a new data source to the project to list the orders in the database.	In the Lab Toolkit, see the following resources: ■ *Northwind Traders Technical Specification: Customer and Customer Order Details Maintenance Components* ■ *Adding a Data Source to a Project* ■ Add a new data source to the project using the Data Source Configuration Wizard with these settings: <table><tr><td>Setting</td><td>Value</td></tr><tr><td>Data source type</td><td>Database</td></tr><tr><td>Data connection</td><td>Microsoft SQL Server</td></tr><tr><td>Server name</td><td>london\sqlexpress.Northwind.dbo</td></tr><tr><td>Connection string</td><td>NorthwindConnectionString</td></tr><tr><td>Database objects</td><td>Stored Procedure: ListOrders</td></tr><tr><td>DataSet name</td><td>NorthwindDataSet</td></tr></table>

(continued)

Tasks	Supporting information
4. Configure the data source to enable inserts, updates, and deletes using existing stored procedures.	In the Lab Toolkit, see the following resources: ■ *Northwind Traders Technical Specification: Customer and Customer Order Details Maintenance Components* ■ *Configuring a Data Component to Use Existing Stored Procedures* ■ In Solution Explorer, double-click **NorthwindDataset.xsd**. ■ Configure the data source that you have just created to use the **ListOrders**, **InsertOrder**, **UpdateOrder**, and **DeleteOrder** stored procedures to maintain the **Orders** table. ■ Make sure you map the stored procedure parameters to the source columns using the information in the Technical Specification. ■ Specify that the wizard should generate a **Fill** and a **GetData** method.
5. Review the wizard - generated code.	■ In Solution Explorer, click **Show all files**. ■ Expand **NorthwindComponent** and then expand **NorthwindDataset.xsd**. If you are programming with Visual C#, open NorthwindDataSet.Designer.cs. If you are programming with Visual Basic, open NorthwindDataSet.Designer.vb. Review the code that the wizard has generated. ■ Notice that the wizard has generated a **ListOrdersTableAdapter** object. ■ Examine the code in the **InitAdapter** method of the **ListOrdersTableAdapter**. This is where the **SelectCommand**, **InsertCommand**, **UpdateCommand**, and **DeleteCommand** objects are configured.
6. Build the Project.	■ Build the NorthwindComponent project, resolving any build errors that occur.
7. Test the display of the orders.	In the Lab Toolkit, see the following resource: *Using a DataGridView with a Data Source Component*. ■ Add a Windows application named **TestHarness** to the solution. ■ Reference the System.Data.dll component (Visual Basic only) and the NorthwindComponent project, and then set the new project to be the StartUp project. **Note** Visual Studio 2005 Beta 2 automatically adds this reference to every new Windows application for C#. ■ Add **using** (C#) / **Imports** (VB) statements for the following libraries to the top of the Form1 code window: • System.Data (VB project only) • System.Data.SqlClient • NorthwindComponent ■ Add a **DataGridView** control to the form

(continued)

Tasks	Supporting information

7. *(continued)*	■ In the Form1 code window, declare and instantiate class members of the following types:
	   ● NorthwindDataSet
	   ● ListOrdersTableAdapter
	■ Add code to the **Form_Load** procedure to display the list of orders in the **DataGridView**.
	■ Use the **Fill** method of your **ListOrdersTableAdapter** object to retrieve the data.
	■ Set the **DataSource** property of the **ListOrdersBindingSource** to the **ListOrders** table in your **NorthwindDataSet** object.
	■ Build the project, resolving any build errors.
	■ Run the project to verify that the order data is displayed.

8. Test the updating of the database.	In the Lab Toolkit, see the following resource: *Using a DataGridView with a Data Source Component.*
	
	■ Add a **Button** control to the form, set the **Text** property to **Update**. Add code to update the underlying database with the changes in the **ListOrders** table in the local **DataSet**.
	■ Build the project, resolving any build errors.
	■ Run the project to verify that it performs as expected by doing the following:
	   ● Run the project.
	   ● Edit the **Quantity** column in the first row and then click the update button.
	   ● Add a row to the end of the table (including valid data for all the columns) and then click the **Update** button.
	   ● Close the application.
	   ● Run the application.
	   ● Verify that the updated quantity and added row are present.
	   ● Delete the last row and then click the **Update** button.
	   ● Close the application.
	   ● Run the application.
	   ● Verify that the added row has now been deleted.

Exercise 2
Creating and Using Stored Procedures with the Data Wizards

In this exercise, you will create and test the **QueriesTableAdapter** component. You will use the TableAdapter Query Configuration Wizard to create and configure this component, which will expose a function named **OrderCost** to your application. This function will internally call the **TotalCostOfOrder** stored procedure in the Northwind database, passing a valid **OrderID**, and return the total cost of that order to the calling application. You will use the TableAdapter Query Configuration Wizard to create the stored procedure in the database.

Scenario

Another requirement of the orders application is to be able to calculate the total cost of a single order. You will generate a query in the component that uses a new stored procedure to calculate this cost.

Tasks	Supporting information
1. Add a new query to the NorthwindDataSet data source.	In the Lab Toolkit, see the following resources: ▪ *Northwind Traders Technical Specification: Customer and Customer Order Details Maintenance Components* ▪ *Adding a Query to a Data Source* ▪ Use the TableAdapter Query Configuration Wizard to create a new query in the project. Use the following information and the Technical Specification to complete the wizard. • Data Connection: NorthwindConnectionString (MySettings) • Command Type: Create new stored procedure • Query Type: SELECT (which returns a single value) **Tip** For this task, you need to edit the **NorthwindDataSet** with the Data Source Designer. Double-click **NorthwindDataSet.xsd** in Solution Explorer to open the Data Source Designer, right-click the designer surface and choose **Add Query**.
2. Build the project.	▪ Build the **NorthwindComponent** project, resolving any build errors that occur.
3. Review the generated code.	▪ In the **Class View** window, expand the NorthwindComponent project and then expand the **NorthwindComponent.NorthwindDataSetTableAdapters** namespace. Notice that a new class has been created named **QueriesTableAdapter**. ▪ Click **QueriesTableAdapter**, and in the lower pane, notice that this class contains an **OrderCost** method. ▪ In Solution Explorer, click **Show all files**. ▪ Open NorthwindDataSet.Designer.cs/NorthwindDataSet.Designer.vb and review the **OrderCost** method of the **QueriesTableAdapter class** that the wizard has generated.

(continued)

Tasks	Supporting information
4. Test the query.	In the Lab Toolkit, see the following resource: *Using a Data Source Query*
	▪ Add a **Button** control to the Windows Form in the test application. Set the **Text** property to **Order Cost**. In the **Click** event handler:
	• Create a local DataGridViewRow variable and set it to the row containing the current cell in the **DataGridView** control.
	Tip You can find the index of the currently selected row using the **DataGridView.CurrentCell.RowIndex** property. Use this value to fetch the current row from the **DataGridView.Rows** collection.
	• Create a local integer variable and name it **OrderID**, and then set it to the value of the first cell in the **DataGridViewRow** that you just created.
	Tip You can identify a single cell in a row using the DataGridRow.Cells collection.
	• Create and instantiate a new **QueriesTableAdapter** object.
	• Call the **OrderCost** method of your **QueriesTableAdapter** object passing the OrderID parameter and displaying the results in a message box.
	▪ Build the project, resolving any build errors.
	▪ Run the project to verify that it functions as expected by doing the following:
	• Run the project.
	• Select any cell in the **DataGridView** control and then click the **Order Cost** button.
	• Verify that the total cost of all items in the order is displayed in a message box.
	• Test the button using different selected cells.

Exercise 3
Using Transact-SQL Statements with the Data Wizards

In this exercise, you will create and test the **ProductsTableAdapter** component. You will use the Data Source Configuration Wizard to create and configure this component, which will expose a **DataSet** of product details to your calling application. Internally, the component will issue a Transact-SQL statement against the Northwind database, passing a **ProductID**, and return the details of a product to the calling application. You will use the Data Source Configuration Wizard to configure the component and Transact-SQL statement.

Scenario

The final requirement for the component is for employees to be able to retrieve information about the products within an order. You need to create a new data component that returns this information from a Transact-SQL statement issued against the Northwind database.

Tasks	Supporting information
1. Add a new data component to the NorthwindDataSet data source.	In the Lab Toolkit, see the following resources: ▪ *Northwind Traders Technical Specification: Customer and Customer Order Details Maintenance Components* ▪ *Adding a Data Component to an Existing Data Source* ▪ Use the TableAdapter Configuration Wizard to create a new data component in the project. Use the following information and the Technical Specification to complete the wizard. • Data Connection: NorthwindConnectionString • Command Type: Use SQL statements **Tip** For this task, you need to edit the **NorthwindDataSet** with the Data Source Designer. Double-click **NorthwindDataSet.xsd** in Solution Explorer to open the Data Source Designer, right-click the designer surface and choose **Add TableAdapter**.
2. Build the project.	▪ Build the **NorthwindComponent** project, resolving any build errors that occur.
3. Review the generated code.	▪ In the **Class View** window, expand the **NorthwindComponent** project, and then expand the **NorthwindComponent** namespace. Note that a new class has been created named **ProductsTableAdapter**. ▪ Click **ProductsTableAdapter**, and in the lower pane, notice that this class contains the standard **Fill** and **Update** methods. ▪ In Solution Explorer, click **Show all files**. ▪ Open NorthwindDataSet.Designer.cs/NorthwindDataSet.Designer.vb and review the code in the **ProductsTableAdapter** class that the wizard has generated.

(continued)

Tasks	Supporting information
4. Test the component.	In the Lab Toolkit, see the following resource: *Using a DataGridView with a Data Source Component.* ■ Add another **Button** control and another **DataGridView** control to the Windows Form in the test application. Set the **Text** property of the Button to **Product Information** and then add code in the **Click** event handler to do the following: • Create a local DataGridViewRow variable and set it to the row containing the current cell in the **DataGridView1** control. • Create a local integer variable and name it **ProductID**, and then set it to the value of the fourth cell in the DataGridViewRow that you just created. • Create and instantiate a new **ProductsTableAdapter** object. • Use the **Fill** method of your **ProductsTableAdapter** to retrieve the data into your existing **NorthwindDataSet** passing the ProductID from the current row as a parameter. • Display the resulting data in the new **DataGridView** control. ■ Build the project, resolving any build errors. ■ Run the project to verify that it functions as expected by doing as follows: • Run the project. • Select any cell in the **DataGridView** control and then click the product information button. • Verify that the second **DataGridView** is populated with the product information for that order. • Test the button using a variety of selected cells.

Lab Discussion

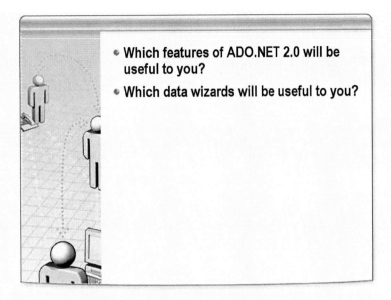

- Which features of ADO.NET 2.0 will be useful to you?
- Which data wizards will be useful to you?

In this lab, you have learned how to use the new data wizards in Visual Studio 2005.

Discuss with the class the advantages that the enhancements to ADO.NET 2.0 will provide for developing applications in your workplace.

Discuss with the class the types of applications in your workplace with which you will be able to use the new data wizards for efficient data access component development.

Workshop Evaluation

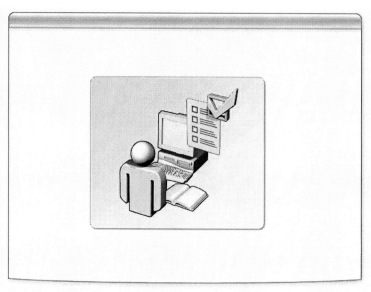

Your evaluation of this workshop will help Microsoft understand the quality of your learning experience.

At a convenient time before the end of the workshop, please complete a workshop evaluation, which is available at http://www.CourseSurvey.com.

Microsoft will keep your evaluation strictly confidential and will use your responses to improve your future learning experience.

Unit 4: Building Presentation Layer Application with Windows Forms

Contents

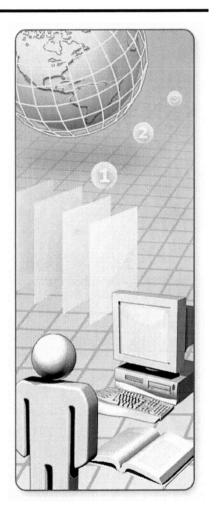

Information in this document, including URL and other Internet Web site references, is subject to change without notice. Unless otherwise noted, the example companies, organizations, products, domain names, e-mail addresses, logos, people, places, and events depicted herein are fictitious, and no association with any real company, organization, product, domain name, e-mail address, logo, person, place or event is intended or should be inferred. Complying with all applicable copyright laws is the responsibility of the user. Without limiting the rights under copyright, no part of this document may be reproduced, stored in or introduced into a retrieval system, or transmitted in any form or by any means (electronic, mechanical, photocopying, recording, or otherwise), or for any purpose, without the express written permission of Microsoft Corporation.

The names of manufacturers, products, or URLs are provided for informational purposes only and Microsoft makes no representations and warranties, either expressed, implied, or statutory, regarding these manufacturers or the use of the products with any Microsoft technologies. The inclusion of a manufacturer or product does not imply endorsement of Microsoft of the manufacturer or product. Links are provided to third party sites. Such sites are not under the control of Microsoft and Microsoft is not responsible for the contents of any linked site or any link contained in a linked site, or any changes or updates to such sites. Microsoft is not responsible for webcasting or any other form of transmission received from any linked site. Microsoft is providing these links to you only as a convenience, and the inclusion of any link does not imply endorsement of Microsoft of the site or the products contained therein.

Microsoft may have patents, patent applications, trademarks, copyrights, or other intellectual property rights covering subject matter in this document. Except as expressly provided in any written license agreement from Microsoft, the furnishing of this document does not give you any license to these patents, trademarks, copyrights, or other intellectual property.

© 2005 Microsoft Corporation. All rights reserved.

Microsoft, ActiveX, IntelliSense, MSDN, MS-DOS, PowerPoint, Visual Basic, Visual C#, Visual SourceSafe, Visual Studio, Visual Web Developer, Windows, Windows Media, Windows NT, and Windows Server are either registered trademarks or trademarks of Microsoft Corporation in the United States and/or other countries.

All other trademarks are property of their respective owners.

Overview

- Enhanced Design-Time Support
- New Controls and Components
- New Data-Binding Model and Features
- Asynchronous Programming
- Other Significant New Features
- Demonstration: RAD Data Binding
- What Is ClickOnce?
- Features and Benefits
- Lab 4A: RAD Data Binding in Windows Forms
- Lab 4B: Data Binding to Components and Web Services
- Lab 4C: Publishing Using ClickOnce
- Discussion

The .NET Framework 2.0 and Microsoft® Visual Studio® 2005 include many new and improved features that enhance the development of Microsoft Windows® Forms applications. This unit begins with an overview of these features and then provides you the opportunity to experiment with some of them. The unit emphasizes the Visual Studio 2005 features most likely to increase productivity when developing Windows Forms applications.

Application deployment and maintenance are a constant challenge to organizations and IT departments. Using ClickOnce, Windows Forms applications can be easily distributed and maintained.

Objectives

After completing this unit, you will be able to:

- Utilize the new design-time features of Visual Studio 2005 to build Windows Forms applications.

- Understand the purpose of the new Windows Forms controls and components included in the .NET Framework 2.0.

- Build highly functional data-bound forms using the Rapid Application Development (RAD) data binding features provided by Visual Studio 2005.

- Perform long-running data retrieval requests while maintaining a responsive Windows Forms interface by using the simplified asynchronous programming capabilities provided by the .NET Framework 2.0.

- Understand the capabilities provided by the new Windows Forms features included in the .NET Framework 2.0 and Visual Studio 2005.

- Describe the purpose of ClickOnce deployment technology.

- List the features of ClickOnce.

- Use ClickOnce to deploy Windows Forms applications.

Enhanced Design-Time Support

- Smart tags
- Snaplines
- In-place editing
- ToolStrip Designer
- Document Outline window

Visual Studio 2005 provides the following new features that simplify the development of Windows Forms applications and improve developer productivity:

■ Smart tags

Smart tags enable you to set properties of a control without leaving the form designer window. They are implemented for some of the standard components in Visual Studio 2005, and you can design your own smart tags for custom components.

At design time, when a control is selected or the mouse hovers over the control, a smart tag anchor is displayed. Clicking the smart tag anchor opens a panel that contains a set of tasks commonly performed on that type of control and possibly a set of commonly edited properties.

■ Snaplines

Snaplines make it a simple task to achieve perfect control positioning without the need to manually edit position properties or run separate processes to position controls.

As you drag controls across the surface of the form designer, dynamically drawn snaplines show useful positional relationships between the control you are moving and other controls nearby on the form. Typical snaplines show the relationship between the edges, margins, padding, and text baselines of controls.

■ In-place editing

Quick Edit Mode enables you to quickly change the string properties of multiple controls on a form.

To enable Quick Edit Mode, right-click on the form designer and click **Property Editing View** from the shortcut menu. This action causes the current Name property of each control on the form to be displayed in an edit control that you can use to view and edit the property. You can access other string properties of the controls by using the **Edit Property** box at the top of the Designer window. To exit Quick Edit Mode, click the **Exit Mode** link at the top of the Designer window.

- ToolStrip Designer

  You can use the ToolStrip Designer to perform in-place editing of menus, toolbars, and status bars.

  The **ToolStrip, MenuStrip, ContextMenuStrip, StatusStrip**, and **ToolStripContainer** controls have replaced previous versions of menus, toolbars, and status bars, and can all be created and edited using the ToolStrip Designer.

- Document Outline window

  The Document Outline window provides a container-oriented view of the controls on a form. To open the Document Outline window, on the **View** menu, point to **Other Windows**, and then click **Document Outline**. You can move controls from one container to another by dragging them to the desired place in the container tree. You can also use this window to delete, cut, copy, paste, and rename controls.

New Controls and Components

- FlowLayoutPanel and TableLayoutPanel controls
- SplitContainer control
- ToolStrip, MenuStrip, StatusStrip, and ContextMenuStrip controls
- DataGridView control
- BindingNavigator control
- MaskedTextBox control
- WebBrowser control

Visual Studio 2005 includes many new Windows Forms controls and components, including:

- **FlowLayoutPanel** and **TableLayoutPanel** controls

    These two new panel controls support the dynamic arrangement of controls at run time. The **FlowLayoutPanel** arranges its contents using a horizontal or vertical flow and the **TableLayoutPanel** arranges its contents in a grid.

- **SplitContainer** control

    This control provides two panels divided by a moveable splitter bar that can be oriented either horizontally or vertically. You can add controls, including the **SplitContainer** control, to either panel. The **SplitContainer** control replaces the **Splitter** control and is more intuitive with better design-time support.

- **ToolStrip**, **MenuStrip**, **StatusStrip**, and **ContextMenuStrip** controls

    These controls replace the previous versions of menus, toolbars, and status bars. They are container controls for hosting toolbar-related items, such as menus, buttons, and text boxes. You can use them to provide intuitive access to important application functionality.

- **DataGridView** control

    The **DataGridView** provides a powerful and flexible solution for displaying data in a tabular format. The data can originate from an external data source or can be stored directly in the control.

- **BindingNavigator** control

    The **BindingNavigator** control provides a VCR-style interface for the navigation and manipulation of data. The **BindingNavigator** is typically used to provide users with a means to control the operation of a **BindingSource** in data-bound Windows Forms applications. This is discussed in more detail later in this unit.

- **MaskedTextBox** control

  This is an enhanced **TextBox** control that uses a mask definition to specify the acceptable structure and format for user input. For example, you can define the precise format for a date or telephone number that a user must enter.

- **WebBrowser** control

  The **WebBrowser** control provides a highly functional Web browser that enables you to incorporate Web pages into your Windows Forms application. It is useful for providing Hypertext Markup Language–based help information and Internet access from within your application.

In addition to these new controls and components, Visual Studio 2005 includes enhancements to many existing controls:

- The **SystemInformation** class has been enhanced to provide access to far more information about the configuration of display options in the current environment.

- The **ListView** and **TreeView** controls now support easier customization through the owner-draw feature similar to that provided by the **ComboBox** and **ListBox**. The **ListView** control now also supports a number of Windows XP and Microsoft Windows Server™ 2003 features.

- New members have been added to important classes including the **Application, Button, ComboBox, Control, Form, Icon, Label, ListBox, MessageBox, RichTextBox, Screen**, and **TextBox** classes. For example, the **Button** control now supports the **MouseOverBackColor** property that you can use to change the button color when the mouse pointer is within the bounds of the control.

New Data Binding Model and Features

- **BindingSource component**
  - Layer of indirection/abstraction between controls and data source
  - Can act as strongly typed data source
  - Interoperates closely with **BindingNavigator** and **DataGridView** controls
- **Data components (concept-not class/component)**
  - Building blocks of typed DataSet
  - Consist of DataTables, TableAdapters, TableAdapter queries
  - Create/edit using DataSet Designer
- **Data sources (concept-not class/component)**
  - Simplified management of data sources
  - Enable drag-and-drop creation of data-bound forms
- **Smart tags**

The .NET Framework 2.0 implements a new data binding model for Windows Forms applications. Visual Studio 2005 provides extensive support for this new data binding model and enables the rapid development of data-bound Windows Forms applications, often through the use of graphical tools. The new components and features include:

- **BindingSource** component

  The **BindingSource** component is central to the new data binding model and is the primary mechanism through which Windows Forms applications access and manipulate data. The **BindingSource** component can act as a conduit to an underlying data source or as a data source in its own right. The **BindingSource** component supports simple and complex data sources, and hides the details of binding contexts and binding managers.

- Data components

  Data components are the logical building block of the typed **DataSet** in Visual Studio 2005. They are not classes. A data component consists of a **DataTable**, a **TableAdapter**, and a set of **TableAdapter** queries. **DataTables** are strongly typed instances of the ADO.NET **DataTable** class. A **TableAdapter** has a similar purpose to a **DataAdapter**, but it also supports the definition of multiple commands or queries that can populate the **DataTable** with any set of data that has the correct schema (or is a single, scalar value).

  You create data components by running the Data Source Configuration Wizard or the Data Component Configuration Wizard from within the **DataSet Designer**. The **DataSet Designer** provides an environment in which you can create and edit typed **DataSets** using visual development tools and wizards. The automated creation of highly functional typed **DataSets** is a huge timesaver for many developers.

- Data sources

  Data sources are a new Visual Studio 2005 concept that allows you to visualize and manage all the sources of data used by your application. A data source can be a database, a file, a Web service, or an object. You create each data source by using the Data Source Configuration Wizard, which requires data-source-specific information. Once created, the source appears as an element in the Data Sources window.

  The key feature of the Data Sources window is that it allows you to graphically configure the elements of a data source (such as a database table and its columns) and drag the data source element onto a form. Visual Studio 2005 automatically creates the controls and components necessary for your code to interact with the data source. The objects created by Visual Studio 2005 depend on the type of data source. For example, dragging a table from a database data source creates a typed **DataSet**, **BindingSource**, and **TableAdapter**, as well as a **BindingNavigator** to facilitate navigation through the data. When using a Web service data source, Visual Studio 2005 will create a proxy class to enable communication with the Web service as opposed to a **BindingSource** and **TableAdapter**.

- Smart tags

  Smart tags play a major role in the implementation of data-bound controls and forms. Data oriented controls such as the **DataGridView** and standard controls that are data-bound provide easy access to data binding features using smart-tag actions. This includes actions such as providing parameters to the query used to display data, and the creation of a Master-Details form from a control. Standard controls, such as the **Label**, **TextBox**, and **ListBox**, that are data bound, also enable you to change the control to a different type of control using smart tag actions.

Asynchronous Programming

- **BackgroundWorker component**
  - DoWork, RunWorkerCompleted, ProgressChanged events
  - RunWorkerAsync, CancelAsync, ReportProgress methods
- **Asynchronous Pattern for Components**
  - Used by .NET Framework components with long-running methods
  - PictureBox has Load and LoadAsync methods, and a LoadCompleted event

Long-running and computer-intensive tasks are always problematic when developing applications with user interfaces. When you launch such a task, either the user interface stops responding to user input until the task completes, or you must use additional threads to run the task as a background process. Unfortunately, multithreaded applications are inherently more complex than single threaded ones, and threading is one of the least understood areas of programming. These factors often lead inexperienced developers to introduce bugs that are extremely difficult to isolate and fix.

The .NET Framework 2.0 and Visual Studio 2005 include two new features that make the development of multithreaded Windows Forms application less complicated:

- **BackgroundWorker** component

  The **BackgroundWorker** component provides an easy-to-use mechanism for executing a method on a background thread, allowing the Windows Forms interface to continue responding to user input.

  You can add a **BackgroundWorker** component from the Toolbox. It will appear in the form's component tray. The **DoWork**, **RunWorkerCompleted**, and **ProgressChanged** events of the **BackgroundWorker** class enable you to specify the code to execute in the background, the code to run when the background method finishes, and the code to run when the **BackgroundWorker** is asked for a progress update. Once the **BackgroundWorker** component is configured, you can use the **RunWorkerAsync** method to start the background thread. The **CancelAsync** method cancels the method running in the background and the **ReportProgress** method can provide status information about the background task.

- Asynchronous Pattern for Components

  The Asynchronous Pattern for Components specifies a pattern to implement when developing components with methods that will potentially take a long time to complete. The pattern stipulates the implementation of methods that run asynchronously and follow a defined naming convention. The .NET Framework components that have long-running methods now implement the Asynchronous Pattern for Components. For example, the **PictureBox** component has a synchronous method named **Load** that can download a picture from a network location. A new method named **LoadAsync** now performs the same operation asynchronously and raises the **LoadCompleted** event when the operation is complete.

Other Significant New Features

* **Application settings**
  * Store application and user preferences on the client
  * Read and write programmatically
* **Double-buffered graphics**
  * Reduces flicker during complex painting operations
  * Set DoubleBuffered property to true

Other significant new Windows Forms features provided by the .NET Framework 2.0 and Visual Studio 2005 include:

■ Application settings.

Application settings make it easy to create, store, and maintain application and user-specific preferences on the client computer. This can include items such as database connection strings, window sizes and positions, and other custom preferences. Settings can be written and read programmatically, as well as bound to control properties at design time.

■ Double-buffered graphics.

Flexible and easy-to-use double-buffering capabilities reduce screen flicker associated with complex painting operations. When double buffering is enabled, all paint operations are first rendered to a memory buffer instead of the drawing surface on the screen. When all paint operations are completed, the memory buffer is copied directly to the drawing surface associated with it. Because only one graphics operation is performed on the screen, the image flickering associated with complex painting operations is eliminated. Default double buffering is enabled by setting a control's **DoubleBuffered** property to **true**. Manual control of double buffering is also possible for more advanced operations through direct manipulation of the **BufferedGraphicsManager** and **BufferedGraphicsContext** classes.

Demonstration: RAD Data Binding

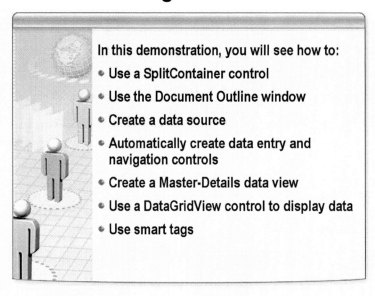

In this demonstration, the instructor will create a data-bound Windows Forms application containing a Master-Details view of the **Customer** and **Orders** tables from the Northwind database. Most importantly, the instructor will create this highly functional application without writing a single line of code.

What Is ClickOnce?

- ClickOnce is a new application deployment technology
- It makes deploying Windows applications as easy as deploying Web applications
- Application updates are easy to administer

Installing client applications has always been difficult and expensive. System administrators must ensure that the application installs reliably on every client, both on initial installation and also whenever the application is updated subsequently.

What Is ClickOnce?

ClickOnce is a new application deployment technology that makes deploying a Windows Forms application as easy as deploying a Web application. With ClickOnce, installing a Windows Forms application is as simple as clicking a link in a Web page. For administrators, deploying or updating an application is simply a matter of updating files on a server.

ClickOnce uses a combination of a set of features in the .NET common language runtime (CLR) and the integrated design-time support in Microsoft Visual Studio 2005. Together, they allow you to create an application that can be automatically installed and updated.

Features and Benefits

* ClickOnce applications are low impact
  * No administrative rights are required on the client machine
* Deployment is through Web servers, CDs, or file systems
* Applications can be installed on the client machine or can run remotely
* ClickOnce applications execute in a secure environment
* Visual Studio provides a rich set of support features for publishing ClickOnce applications
* Prerequisite software can be installed alongside the application installation

ClickOnce is the recommended approach for publishing applications developed using Visual Studio 2005.

ClickOnce Features and Benefits

ClickOnce provides a number of features and benefits, described as follows:

- ClickOnce applications are low-impact. Applications are installed per user, meaning that for application installation and updates, no administrative rights are required.

- These applications can be deployed through a Web server, a Universal Naming Convention (UNC) file share, or by CD.

- ClickOnce offers two installation options:

  - *Installed applications.* The application copies to the client machine. It can be started from the Windows **Start** menu, and removed through the **Add/Remove Programs** option on the Control Panel on the client machine.

  - *Launched applications.* The application does not install onto the client machine but copies from the server and runs directly.

- ClickOnce applications run in a secure sandbox provided by the CLR Code Access Security model. Visual Studio helps the developer, author for the sandbox with features such as F5 Debug in Security Zone and a code-analysis tool that determines an application's required permissions.

- Visual Studio 2005 offers rich support for publishing applications using ClickOnce. The Publish page in the application properties allows a developer to specify the publishing location, version information, which files to include, dependencies and prerequisite software, and whether the deployed application should periodically check for updates.

- A prerequisite for all ClickOnce applications is that the target client must have the .NET Framework 2.0 installed. Visual Studio 2005 generates a bootstrapper file that automatically installs all the specified prerequisites (including the .NET Framework) when the application first installs. Note that if the .NET Framework needs to be installed, the account used on the remote client must have administrative privileges.

Lab 4A: RAD Data Binding in Windows Forms

- Exercise 1: Displaying Master Data Using RAD Data Binding
- Exercise 2: Displaying Details Data Using RAD Data Binding
- Exercise 3: Parameterizing Data Component Queries
- Exercise 4: Editing DataSets Using the DataSet Designer

After completing this lab, you will be able to:

- Create Windows Forms applications using the new data binding model in Visual Studio 2005.
- Create data-bound forms using the RAD data binding features of Visual Studio 2005.
- Use smart tags to perform common actions on controls.
- Use the **Document Outline** view to organize control hierarchies.
- Parameterize the queries used by a data component.
- Modify the structure of a **DataSet** using the **DataSet Designer**.
- Use some of the important new controls and components, including the **BindingSource**.
- **DataGridView**, **BindingNavigator**, **SplitContainer**, and **ToolStrip**.

 Important You can choose to perform this workshop using either Microsoft Visual C#® or Microsoft Visual Basic®. Code samples and lab solutions are provided in both programming languages. If you prefer, you can choose to perform some labs using one programming language, and perform others using the other language. However, once you start a lab, you should complete all the lab exercises using the same programming language.

Lab Setup

For this lab, you will use the LONDON Virtual PC.

To prepare for this lab:

1. If LONDON is still running after the previous lab, on the **Action** menu, click **Close**. The **Action** menu is visible when the Virtual PC is running in windowed mode, but not when it is running full-screen. If you are running the Virtual PC full-screen, press <RIGHT>ALT+ENTER to switch to windowed mode.

2. In the Close window, select **Turn off and delete changes** and then click **OK**.

3. Start LONDON Virtual PC.

4. Log on as **Student** with a password of **Pa$$w0rd**.

5. Click the **Labfiles** Toolbar at the bottom right of the screen, and navigate to the Lab04a\Setup folder.

6. Click the **Install** file to set up the Virtual PC for this lab.

7. Enter the Administrator's password when prompted, which is **Pa$$w0rd**.

8. Press any key to exit the setup command procedure.

 Caution The setup procedure for this lab performs operations with the SQL Server. If you have recently started the virtual PC, the database server may not have completed its startup. If you run the install script and you see either of the following errors, wait a few minutes and then try to run the install script again:

- Client unable to establish connection

- Shared Memory Provider: The system cannot find the file specified.

- Timeout expired.

 Important The sample Northwind data provided for this lab creates orders only for suppliers numbered 1, 4, and 7. This means that when you test the application developed in this lab, only orders and order details for these suppliers will appear. Order information for all other suppliers will be blank.

Lab Toolkit Resources

Use the following resources in the Lab Toolkit to help you complete this lab:

- Northwind Traders Technical Specification: Supplier and Supplier Details Maintenance Application

- Creating Data Sources Using the Data Source Configuration Wizard

- Creating Data-Bound Windows Forms from Data Sources

- Using Smart Tags to Perform Common Configuration Tasks

- Creating Master-Details Data-Bound Forms

- Editing DataSets Using the DataSet Designer

- Parameterizing Queries Using the Search Criteria Builder

Estimated time to complete this lab: **75 minutes**

Lab Solution Files

There are Visual Basic and Visual C# solution files associated with the labs in this workshop. The lab solution files are located in the folder E:\Microsoft Learning\2364\Labfiles\Lab04a\Solution on the Virtual PCs.

Exercise 1
Displaying Master Data Using RAD Data Binding

In this exercise, you will study the Technical Specification document that describes the details of the application you must build. You will create the first part of the application: a form that displays the data from the **Suppliers** table in a series of **Label** and **TextBox** controls and which provides a VCR-like navigation control to move through supplier records.

Scenario

You decide to approach the development of the Supplier Order Detail Maintenance application by implementing one **DataSet** at a time, beginning with the **Suppliers** table. Once you have the basic application working correctly, accessing data from the **Suppliers** table, you will extend the application to handle data from the **Supplier Orders** and finally the **Supplier Order Details** tables.

Tasks	Supporting information
1. Open the Lab Toolkit and read the Technical Specification for the Supplier Maintenance application.	See the resource in the Lab Toolkit, *Northwind Traders Technical Specification: Supplier and Supplier Details Maintenance Application.*
2. Start Visual Studio 2005 and create a new Windows Application project using the language of your choice (either Visual Basic or Visual C#). Name the project **NorthwindSuppliers**.	▪ Create a Windows Application project using the following settings: • Template: **Windows Application** • Name: **NorthwindSuppliers**
3. Configure the application's main form.	▪ Set the following properties of the application's main form to the values specified: • (Name): **Suppliers** • Text: **Suppliers** • Size: **850, 500** • BackColor: **Lavender** (from the Web color pallet)
4. Configure the layout of the main form.	▪ Divide the Suppliers form vertically by dragging a **SplitContainer** control from the **Toolbox**, under Containers, and then dropping it onto the Suppliers form. Notice how the **SplitContainer** control: • Automatically fills the entire Suppliers form. • Provides a split view of the form at design time. ▪ Change the appearance of the **SplitContainer1** control by setting the following properties to the specified values: • BorderStyle: **FixedSingle** • SplitterDistance: **300**

(continued)

Tasks	Supporting information
5. Create a new data source containing the **Suppliers** and **Supplier Orders** tables from the Northwind database.	See the following resources in the Lab Toolkit: ▪ *Northwind Traders Technical Specification: Supplier and Supplier Details Maintenance Application* ▪ *Creating Data Sources Using the Data Source Configuration Wizard* ▪ On the **Data** menu, click **Add New Data Source** to run the Data Source Configuration Wizard. Use the following settings to configure the new data source: • Data source type: **Database** • Data source: **Microsoft SQL Server** • Server name: **london\sqlexpress** • Database name: **Northwind** • Connection name: **NorthwindConnectionString** • Save connection string: **Yes** • Database objects included: **Suppliers** and **Supplier Orders** tables • DataSet name: **NorthwindDataSet**
6. Configure the **Suppliers** table in the new **NorthwindDataSet** data source to generate a set of Windows Forms controls.	See the following resources in the Lab Toolkit: ▪ *Northwind Traders Technical Specification: Supplier and Supplier Details Maintenance Application* ▪ *Creating Data-Bound Windows Forms from Data Sources* ▪ On the **Data** menu, click **Show Data Sources** to display the Data Sources window. In the Data Sources window: • Configure the **Suppliers** table to generate a **Details** view instead of the default grid. • Configure the SupplierID field to generate a **Label** control. • Drag the **Suppliers** table and drop it onto **SplitContainer1.Panel1** on the Suppliers form. • Ensure that the controls are displayed as shown in the Technical Specification.
7. Remove the functionality to add and delete suppliers.	See the following resources in the Lab Toolkit: ▪ *Northwind Traders Technical Specification: Supplier and Supplier Details Maintenance Application* ▪ *Using Smart Tags to Perform Common Configuration Tasks* ▪ To Control the operations available on supplier data, right-click the **SuppliersBindingNavigator** control and click Edit Items. ▪ In the **Items Collection Editor** dialog box, delete the **bindingNavigatorAddNewItem** and **bindingNavigatorDeleteItem** items.

(continued)

Tasks	Supporting information
8. Enable the saving of supplier data.	■ To enable the user to save modifications to the supplier data: ● Verify that the **Enabled** property of the **bindingNavigatorSaveItem** is set to **true**.
9. Build the project.	■ Build the **NorthwindSuppliers** solution, resolving any build errors that occur.

10. Test the application.	■ Run the **NorthwindSuppliers** application and confirm that:
	   ● The layout of the application created so far is consistent with that shown in the Technical Specification.
	   ● The program allows navigation through records in the **Suppliers** table.
	   ● All fields apart from the **SupplierID** can be edited.
	   ● You can save modified data but cannot add or delete records.

Exercise 2
Displaying Details Data Using RAD Data Binding

In this exercise, you will use a **DataGridView** to display all the orders associated with the currently displayed supplier.

Scenario

Having successfully implemented the functionality required to interact with the **Suppliers** table, you must now turn your attention to the **Supplier Orders** table. As the user navigates through each supplier record, the application must display a list of orders associated with the supplier.

Tasks	Supporting information
1. Modify the layout of the main form.	▪ Divide **SplitContainer1.Panel2** on the **Suppliers** form by dragging a **SplitContainer** control from the **Toolbox** and dropping it onto the form. Configure the appearance of the **SplitContainer2** control by changing the following properties to the specified values: • BorderStyle: **FixedSingle** • Orientation: **Horizontal** • SplitterDistance: **250**
2. Create the Supplier Orders grid.	▪ Drag the **Supplier Orders** table that is a child of the **Suppliers** table from the Data Sources window and drop it in the top panel of the **SplitContainer2** control. This creates a DataViewGrid which displays the supplier order related to the master record.
3. Configure the content of the Supplier Orders grid.	See the following resources in the Lab Toolkit: ▪ *Northwind Traders Technical Specification: Supplier and Supplier Details Maintenance Application* ▪ *Using Smart Tags to Perform Common Configuration Tasks* ▪ The default **DataGridView** generated by Visual Studio 2005 displays all data columns from the **Supplier Order** table. To remove the **SupplierID** column, right-click **Supplier_OrdersDataGridView** and then click **Edit Columns**. • In the **DataGridView** control's **Edit Columns** dialog box, delete the **SupplierID** column.

(continued)

Tasks	Supporting information
4. Configure the behavior and appearance of the supplier orders grid.	See the following resources in the Lab Toolkit: • *Northwind Traders Technical Specification: Supplier and Supplier Details Maintenance Application* • *Using Smart Tags to Perform Common Configuration Tasks* ■ Use the new **DataGridView** control's smart tag to perform the following: • Disable adding of rows. • Disable editing of rows. • Disable deletion of rows. • Enable column reordering. • Dock in parent container.
5. Modify additional properties of the supplier orders grid.	■ Smart tags provide access only to the most commonly used configuration tasks and settings. It is often necessary to configure properties using the Properties window. Use the Properties window for the **Supplier_OrdersDataGridView** to configure the following properties: • MultiSelect: **False** • SelectionMode: **FullRowSelect**
6. Build the project.	■ Build the **NorthwindSuppliers** solution, resolving any build errors that occur.
7. Test the application.	■ Execute the **NorthwindSuppliers** application and confirm that: • The application now displays all supplier records and matching orders for the current supplier (for suppliers 1, 4, and 7). • The **Supplier Orders** grid is read-only. • Clicking anywhere on a row in the **supplier orders** grid highlights the entire row. • The columns can be resized. • The **Supplier Orders** can be sorted based on any value by clicking the column header.

Exercise 3
Parameterizing Data Component Queries

In this exercise, you will parameterize database queries to retrieve subsets of the supplier orders data based on the order's state of completion. You will provide access to these queries through a set of buttons on a **ToolStrip** control, allowing the user to filter supplier orders.

Scenario

Over time, the number of orders recorded against each supplier will grow. Eventually, the application will need to provide full searching and filtering functionality. However, in the interests of delivering a solution quickly it has been decided that it is sufficient for now if the application allows the user to filter by the state of a supplier order.

Tasks	Supporting information

1. Parameterize the Supplier Orders query.	See the resource in the Lab Toolkit, *Parameterizing Queries Using the Search Criteria Builder*.
	
	■ Parameterize the **DataGridView** data sources using the **Search Criteria Builder** dialog box. Select the **DataGridView** control on the form, click the **Data** menu, and then click **Add Query**.
	
	   • Set the data source table to **NorthwindDataSet.Supplier Orders**.
	
	   • Add the following **Transact-SQL WHERE** clause to the end of the existing query:
	
	   `WHERE State = @Filter`

2. Test the application.	■ Run the **NorthwindSuppliers** application and confirm that:
	
	   • A new **ToolStrip** control has been added to the form containing the **DataGridView**.
	
	   • When you enter an integer between 0 and 3 in the **Filter** box and click **FillBy**, the rows are filtered to display only relevant records. Note that the filter is applied to all rows of the child table, and when another row is selected, the filter is still effective.

Exercise 4
Editing DataSets Using the DataSet Designer

In this exercise, you will use the DataSet Designer to edit the **NorthwindDataSet** class. You will manually create a data component that creates a table named **Supplier Order Details** and populates it with data joined from the **Supplier Order Details** and **Products** tables in the Northwind database. You will use this new table to show the user details of the products contained on individual supplier orders.

Scenario

The final step in the development of the Supplier Maintenance application is to display the individual items contained on each order. However, to obtain meaningful data, you must join the **Supplier Order Details** table with the **Products** table. There are many ways to approach this problem, but you will minimize the coding required by using the new DataSet Designer.

Tasks	Supporting information
1. Create a new data component.	See the resource in the Lab Toolkit, *Editing DataSets Using the DataSet Designer*.
	▪ Open the **NorthwindDataSet.xsd** schema in the **DataSet Designer**.
	▪ Add a new Query to the DataSet by using the following information:
	• Data connection: **NorthwindConnectionString(Settings)**
	• Command type: **Use SQL statements**
	• Query type : **SELECT which returns a single value**
	• SQL Statement: **SELECT Products.ProductName, [Supplier Order Details].SupplierOrderID, [Supplier Order Details].ProductID, [Supplier Order Details].UnitsOnOrder, [Supplier Order Details].UnitsReceived, [Supplier Order Details].ReceivedDate FROM Products INNER JOIN [Supplier Order Details] ON Products.ProductID = [Supplier Order Details].ProductID**
	• Function Name: **ScalarQuery**
	Tip simpler way to do this is to drag the **Supplier Orders Detail** table and **Products** table, from the Server Explorer window onto the **Dataset Designer**. Then use the TableAdapter Configuration Wizard to apply the above settings. It is necessary to change the name of the **Data Table** in the properties window by using this method. This technique automatically creates the relation in the following step.
2. Create a new parent-child relation between the **Supplier Orders** and **Supplier Order Details** tables.	▪ Add a new relation to the **DataSet** using the following information:
	• Parent Table: **Supplier Orders**.
	• Child Table: **Supplier Order Details**.
	• Notice the new link between the **Supplier Orders** and **Supplier Order Details** tables that represents the relation you just created.
	▪ Build the solution to ensure that Visual Studio can generate the Master-Details view created in the next step.

(*continued*)

Tasks	Supporting information
3. Create the Order Details grid	▪ From the **Data Sources** window, drag the **Supplier Order Details** Data Table, and drop it on to the lower panel of **SplitContainer2**.
4. Configure the content of the supplier orders grid.	See the following resources in the Lab Toolkit: ▪ *Northwind Traders Technical Specification: Supplier and Supplier Details Maintenance Application* ▪ *Using Smart Tags to Perform Common Configuration Tasks* ▪ In the **DataGridView** control's **Edit Columns** dialog box, perform the following actions: • Delete the **SupplierOrderID** column. • Place the remaining columns in the following order: **ProductID, ProductName, UnitsOnOrder, UnitsReceived, ReceivedDate**.
5. Modify the behavior and appearance of the order details grid.	See the resource in the Lab Toolkit, *Northwind Traders Technical Specification: Supplier and Supplier Details Maintenance Application*. ▪ Use the new **DataGridView** control's smart tag to perform the following actions: • Disable adding of rows. • Disable editing of rows. • Disable deletion of rows. • Enable column reordering. • Dock in parent container.
6. Change additional properties of the order details grid.	See the resource in the Lab Toolkit, *Northwind Traders Technical Specification: Supplier and Supplier Details Maintenance Application*. ▪ Use the Properties Window for the **Supplier Order DetailsDataGridView** to configure the following properties: • MultiSelect: **False** • SelectionMode: **FullRowSelect**
7. Build the project.	▪ Build the **NorthwindSuppliers** solution, resolving any build errors that occur.
8. Test the application.	▪ Run the **NorthwindSuppliers** application and confirm that: • The application now displays the products contained in the currently selected supplier order. • The order details grid displays data obtained from both the **Products** and **Supplier Order Details** tables.

Lab 4B: Data Binding to Components and Web Services

- Exercise 1: Connecting the Client Tier to the Middle Tier
- Exercise 2: Consuming a Web Service Data Source
- Exercise 3: Implementing Asynchronous Calls to a Web Service Data Source

After completing this lab, you will be able to:

- Reuse data binding components in business-tier objects.
- Create data-bound forms that bind to business objects.
- Create data-bound forms that bind to data exposed by a Web service.
- Program the asynchronous methods of a Web service to perform long-running tasks on a background thread.

 Important You can choose to program with either Visual C# or Visual Basic in this workshop. Code samples and lab solutions are provided in both programming languages. If you prefer, you can choose to perform some labs using one programming language, and perform others using the other language. However, once you start a lab, you should complete all lab exercises using the same programming language.

Lab Setup

For this lab, you will use the LONDON Virtual PC.

To prepare for this lab:

1. If LONDON is still running after the previous lab, on the **Action** menu, click **Close**. The **Action** menu is visible when the Virtual PC is running in windowed mode, but not when it is running full-screen. If you are running the Virtual PC full-screen, press <RIGHT>ALT+ENTER to switch to windowed mode.

2. In the Close window, select **Turn off and delete changes** and then click **OK**.

3. Start LONDON Virtual PC.

4. Log on as **Student** with a password of **Pa$$w0rd**.

5. Click the **Labfiles** Toolbar at the bottom right of the screen, and navigate to the **Lab04b\Setup** folder.

6. Click the **Install** file to set up the Virtual PC for this lab.

7. Enter the Administrator's password when prompted, which is **Pa$$w0rd**.

8. Press any key to exit the setup command procedure.

 Caution The setup procedure for this lab performs operations with the SQL Server. If you have recently started the virtual PC, the database server may not have completed its startup. If you run the install script and you see either of the following errors, wait a few minutes and then try to run the install script again:

- Client unable to establish connection
- Shared Memory Provider: The system cannot find the file specified.
- Timeout expired.

Lab Toolkit Resources

Use the following Lab Toolkit resources to help you complete this lab:

- Northwind Traders Technical Specification: Suppliers Application v2
- Northwind Traders Technical Specification: Orders Application
- Exposing a Data Source from a Web Service
- Using a Web Service Data Source
- Asynchronous Calls Using a Web Service Data Source

Estimated time to complete this lab: **90 minutes**

Lab Solution Files

There are Visual Basic and Visual C# solution files associated with the labs in this workshop. The lab solution files are located in the folder E:\Microsoft Learning\2364\Labfiles\Lab04b\Solution on the Virtual PCs.

Exercise 1
Connecting the Client Tier to the Middle Tier

In this exercise you will convert the two-tier application created in the previous lab to use the three tier model. You will update the client-tier application to use .NET Remoting to obtain data from the middle-tier components. You will bind the Windows Forms components to objects acting as data sources, rather than connecting directly to the database from the Windows Forms application.

Scenario

The first version of the Supplier Maintenance application is not scalable. You have been asked to implement a version of the application that will support a large number of users. Therefore, you have decided to migrate the components that connect to the database to a middle-tier server application executing close to the database server, and to implement components on the client that communicate with the middle tier. In this way, the same middle-tier objects can service many clients simultaneously if required.

Because this is not a trivial task, you have been asked to build a simple version of the application as an initial proof-of-concept. This version of the application just provides access to the suppliers' details, and not to the orders. If this version of the application is successful, you plan to migrate the remainder of the functionality at a later date.

The server application has already been developed and consists of three projects:

- NorthwindServerInterface, defining the methods and objects exposed by the remoting server. This project will be compiled into a dynamic-link library (DLL) assembly that will need to be deployed to each client computer as well as the server computer.

- NorthwindService, containing a class that implements the methods in the NorthwindServerInterface project. This will also be compiled into a library assembly but needs to be deployed only to the server computer.

- NorthwindServer, containing the remoting server application hosting the objects accessed by clients. This will be compiled as an executable assembly (EXE) and deployed to the server computer.

Tasks	Supporting information
1. Open the Lab Toolkit and read the Technical Specification for the Suppliers application.	See the resource on the Scenario tab in the Lab Toolkit, *Northwind Traders Technical Specification: Suppliers Application v2.*
2. Start Visual Studio 2005 and open the NorthwindSuppliers solution.	▪ Open the **NorthwindSuppliers** solution from E:\Microsoft Learning\ 2364\Labfiles\Lab04b\Starter\CS or E:\Microsoft Learning\2364\ Labfiles\Lab04b\Starter\VB. Notice that this solution contains the projects that implement the .NET Remoting server that are listed in the Scenario description for this exercise.
3. Add a new Windows Application project to the NorthwindSuppliers solution and name it **NorthwindClient**.	▪ Add a Windows Application project using the following settings: • Template: **Windows Application** • Name: **NorthwindClient**
4. Configure the application's main form.	▪ Set the following properties of the application's main form to the values specified: • (Name): **Suppliers** • BackColor: **Lavender** (from the Web color pallet) • Size: **300, 500** • Text: **Suppliers**
5. Add a new class to the application and name it **Supplier**.	▪ The **Supplier** class will be used as the data source for the client application. It will be instantiated and populated with data retrieved from the NorthwindServer remoting server. ▪ In the NorthwindClient project, add a new class and name it **Supplier**.
6. Define properties for the **Supplier** class.	▪ Classes used as data sources must expose data values as properties. ▪ Add the following private variables to the **Supplier** class: ```//C#\nprivate int supplierID;\nprivate string companyName;\nprivate string contactName;\nprivate string contactTitle;\nprivate string address;\n\n'Visual Basic\nPrivate _supplierID As Integer\nPrivate _companyName As String\nPrivate _contactName As String\nPrivate _contactTitle As String\nPrivate _address As String```

(continued)

Tasks	Supporting information
6. *(continued)*	■ Add the following public property definitions to the **Supplier** class:

```csharp
//C#
public int SupplierID
{
    get { return supplierID; }
}

public string CompanyName
{
    get { return companyName; }
    set { companyName = value; }
}

public string ContactName
{
    get { return contactName; }
    set { contactName = value; }
}
public string ContactTitle
{
    get { return contactTitle; }
    set { contactTitle = value; }
}

public string Address
{
    get { return address; }
    set { address = value; }
}
```

```vbnet
'Visual Basic
Public ReadOnly Property SupplierID() As Integer
 Get
    Return _supplierID
 End Get
End Property

Public Property CompanyName() As String
 Get
    Return _companyName
 End Get
  Set(ByVal value As String)
    _companyName = value
 End Set
End Property
```

(Code continued on the following page.)

(continued)

Tasks	Supporting information

6. *(continued)*	```vb
	Public Property ContactName() As String
	 Get
	    Return _contactName
	 End Get
	  Set(ByVal value As String)
	    _contactName = value
	 End Set
	End Property
	
	Public Property ContactTitle() As String
	 Get
	    Return _contactTitle
	 End Get
	  Set(ByVal value As String)
	    _contactTitle = value
	 End Set
	End Property
	Public Property Address() As String
	 Get
	    Return _address
	 End Get
	  Set(ByVal value As String)
	    _address = value
	 End Set
	End Property
	``
	
	📄 **Note** The SupplierID property is read-only.

(continued)

Tasks	Supporting information
7. Define the constructor.	▪ The **Supplier** class requires a constructor to populate its data. ▪ Add the following constructor to the **Supplier** class: ```cpp\n//C#\npublic Supplier(int ID, string compName, string\ncontName, string contTitle, string addr)\n{\n supplierID = ID;\n companyName = compName;\n contactName = contName;\n contactTitle = contTitle;\n address = addr;\n}\n\n'Visual Basic\nPublic Sub New(ByVal ID As Integer, ByVal _\n compName As String, ByVal contName As String, _\n ByVal contTitle As String, ByVal addr As String)\n _supplierID = ID\n _companyName = compName\n _contactName = contName\n _contactTitle = contTitle\n _address = addr\nEnd Sub\n``` ▪ Build the **NorthwindClient** project.
8. Create a new data source based on the **Supplier** class.	▪ Display the **Suppliers** form in the Designer view. ▪ On the **Data** menu, click **Add New Data Source** to run the Data Source Configuration Wizard. Use the following settings to configure the new data source: • Data source type: **Object** • Object location: **NorthwindClient.Supplier**
9. Configure the Supplier data source to generate a set of Windows Forms controls.	▪ Make the **Suppliers** form [Design] the current window. ▪ On the **Data** menu, click **Show Data Sources** to display the Data Sources window. In the **Data Sources** window: • Configure the **Supplier** data source to generate a Details view instead of the default grid. • Configure the **SupplierID** field to generate a Label control. • Drag the **Supplier** data source and drop it onto the **Suppliers** form. • Position the controls on the form appropriately, with the **SupplierID** at the top, as shown in the Technical Specification for the Suppliers application. See the resource on the Scenario tab in the Lab Toolkit, *Northwind Traders Technical Specification: Suppliers Application v2*.

(continued)

Tasks	Supporting information
10. Remove the functionality to add and delete suppliers.	■ Control the operations available on supplier data by configuring the **supplierBindingNavigator** control as follows: • In the **Items Collection Editor**, delete the **bindingNavigatorAddNewItem** and **bindingNavigatorDeleteItem** items.

11. Create the configuration file for the **NorthwindClient** project.	■ The configuration settings defining the location of the remoting server should be held in an application configuration file. Use the Application Configuration File template to add a file to the **NorthwindClient** project and name it app.config.
	
	■ Edit the app.config file and add the following entries. These entries specify the port and protocol that the client will use to connect to the server:
	<pre><system.runtime.remoting>
	  <application>
	    <channels>
	      <channel ref="tcp" />
	    </channels>
	    <client>
	      <wellknown
	type="NorthwindServerInterface.ISupplierInfo,
	NorthwindServerInterface"
	url="tcp://localhost:6000/SupplierInfo.rem" />
	    </client>
	  </application>
	</system.runtime.remoting></pre>

12. Add the code to retrieve the supplier data from the remoting server.	■ Add references to the **System.Runtime.Remoting.dll** and **NorthwindServerInterface.dll** assemblies to the **NorthwindClient** project.
	
	■ Display the source code for Form1 in the Code View window (if you are using Visual Basic, edit the file Form1.Designer.vb). Add **Imports/using** statements for the **System.Runtime.Remoting** and **NorthwindServerInterface** namespaces.
	
	■ If you are using Visual C#, add a **using** statement for the **NorthwindSuppliers** namespace.
	
	■ If you are using Visual Basic, add a reference to the System.Data.dll assembly, and an **Imports** statement for the **System.Data** namespace.
	
	■ Add a private variable to the **Suppliers** class and name it **northwindDS**, as follows:
	<pre>//C#
	private NorthwindSuppliers.NorthwindDataSet
	northwindDS;
	
	'Visual Basic
	Private northwindDS As NorthwindDataSet</pre>

(continued)

Tasks	Supporting information

12. *(continued)*	▪ Add the following statements that connect to the remoting server, retrieve the supplier data, and populate the **supplierBindingSource**, to end of the constructor:
	
	Note If you are using Visual Basic you may need to create the constructor before adding the following code.
	
	```csharp\n//C#\n\n// Connect to the server\nRemotingConfiguration.Configure("..\\..\\app.config");\nWellKnownClientTypeEntry[] entry =\nRemotingConfiguration.GetRegisteredWellKnownClientTypes\n();\nISupplierInfo suppData =\n(ISupplierInfo)Activator.GetObject(entry[0].ObjectType,\nentry[0].ObjectUrl);\n\n// Retrieve the DataSet\nnorthwindDS = suppData.SupplierInfo;\n\n// Populate the BindingSource\nforeach (DataRow dr in northwindDS.Tables[0].Rows)\n{\n Supplier sp = new Supplier((int)dr[0],\n(string)dr[1], (string)dr[2], (string)dr[3],\n(string)dr[4]);\n supplierBindingSource.Add(sp);\n}\n```
	```vbnet\n'Visual Basic\n\n' Connect to the server\n\nRemotingConfiguration.Configure("..\\..\\app.config")\nDim entry() As WellKnownClientTypeEntry = _\nRemotingConfiguration.GetRegisteredWellKnownClientTypes\n()\nDim suppData As ISupplierInfo = _\n Activator.GetObject(entry(0).ObjectType, _\n entry(0).ObjectUrl)\n\n' Retrieve the DataSet\nnorthwindDS = suppData.SupplierInfo\n\n' Populate the BindingSource\nFor Each dr As DataRow In northwindDS.Tables(0).Rows\n Dim sp As Supplier = New Supplier(CInt(dr(0)), _\n CStr(dr(1)), CStr(dr(2)), CStr(dr(3)), CStr(dr(4)))\n SupplierBindingSource.Add(sp)\nNext\n```

(continued)

Tasks	Supporting information
13. Add code to record changes made by the user.	▪ Create an event handler for the **KeyUp** event for the **Address**, **CompanyName**, **ContactName**, and **ContactTitle** text boxes. **Tip** If you select all the text boxes, you can create a single event handler for them all. ▪ The event handler should save the changes made to the current row back to the **DataSet**:

```
//C#

int currentRowIndex =
Int32.Parse(bindingNavigatorPositionItem.Text) - 1;
DataRow currentRow =
northwindDS.Tables[0].Rows[currentRowIndex];

currentRow.BeginEdit();
currentRow[1]  = companyNameTextBox.Text;
currentRow[2]  = contactNameTextBox.Text;
currentRow[3]  = contactTitleTextBox.Text;
currentRow[4]  = addressTextBox.Text;
currentRow.EndEdit();
'Visual Basic
Dim currentRowIndex As Integer = _
 Int32.Parse(bindingNavigatorPositionItem.Text) - 1
Dim currentRow As System.Data.DataRow = _
 northwindDS.Tables(0).Rows(currentRowIndex)

currentRow.BeginEdit()
currentRow(1) = CompanyNameTextBox.Text
currentRow(2) = ContactNameTextBox.Text
currentRow(3) = ContactTitleTextBox.Text
currentRow(4) = AddressTextBox.Text
currentRow.EndEdit()
```

(continued)

Tasks	Supporting information
14. Add the code to save changes back to the database.	■ To enable the user to save modifications to the supplier data: ● In the Properties window, set the **Enabled** property of the **BindingNavigatorSaveItem** in the **supplierBindingNavigator** toolstrip on the form to **true**. ● Create an event handler for the **Click** event of the **BindingNavigatorSaveItem** control and add code to send the data back to the remoting server: <pre>//C#

// Connect to the server again
WellKnownClientTypeEntry[] entry =
RemotingConfiguration.GetRegisteredWellKnownClientTypes
();
ISupplierInfo suppData =
(ISupplierInfo)Activator.GetObject(entry[0].ObjectType,
entry[0].ObjectUrl);

// Send the DataSet back to the server
suppData.SaveSupplierInfo(northwindDS);
northwindDS.AcceptChanges();

'Visual Basic
' Connect to the server again
Dim entry() As WellKnownClientTypeEntry = _
RemotingConfiguration.GetRegisteredWellKnownClientTypes
()
Dim suppData As ISupplierInfo = _
 Activator.GetObject(entry(0).ObjectType, _
 entry(0).ObjectUrl)

' Send the DataSet back to the server
suppData.SaveSupplierInfo(northwindDS)
northwindDS.AcceptChanges()</pre> |
| **15.** Build the project. | ■ Build the **NorthwindSuppliers** solution, resolving any build errors that occur. |

(continued)

Tasks	Supporting information
16. Run the server application.	▪ Open a command prompt window. If you are using Visual C#, change to the E:\Microsoft Learning\2364\Labfiles\Lab04b\Starter\CS\ NorthwindServer\bin\Debug folder. If you are using Visual Basic, change to the E:\Microsoft Learning\2364\Labfiles\Lab04b\Starter\ VB\NorthwindServer\bin folder. ▪ Verify that this folder contains the assemblies NorthwindServer.exe, NorthwindServerInterface.dll, and NorthwindService.dll. ▪ Execute the NorthwindServer.exe application. The message "Server running. Press Enter to terminate" will appear. (Do not press ENTER yet.) **Note** You will receive a Windows Security Alert informing you that the firewall has blocked some features of the program, if the firewall is active. This is not an issue unless the service is accessed from outside the firewall, which is not the case for the NorthwindServer service.
17. Test the client application.	▪ Open another command prompt window. If you are using Visual C#, change to the E:\Microsoft Learning\2364\Labfiles\Lab04b\Starter\CS\ NorthwindClient\bin\Debug folder. If you are using Visual Basic, change to the E:\Microsoft Learning\ 2364\Labfiles\Lab04b\Starter\VB\NorthwindClient\bin\Debug folder. ▪ Verify that this folder contains the assemblies NorthwindClient.exe and NorthwindServerInterface.dll. (NorthwindService.dll should not be present.) ▪ Run the NorthwindClient.exe application, and confirm that: • The program allows navigation through records in the **Suppliers** table. • All fields apart from the SupplierID are editable. • You can save modified data but cannot add or delete records.

Exercise 2
Consuming a Web Service Data Source

In this exercise, you will create a Windows Form application that consumes the Web service you have just created. You will display the returned **DataSet** in a **DataGridView** control.

Scenario

You have been asked to create a simple Windows Form application that will display the Order Details information in a grid view.

Tasks	Supporting information
1. Open the Lab Toolkit and read the Technical Specification for the Orders application.	See the resource on the Scenario tab in the Lab Toolkit, *Northwind Traders Technical Specification: Orders Application.*
2. Create a Windows Form application.	<ul><li>Add a new Windows application to the solution using the following settings:<ul><li>Template: **Windows Application**</li><li>Name: **OrdersClient**</li><li>Location: **C:\Documents and Settings\Student\My Documents\Visual Studio 2005\Projects**</li></ul></li><li>Set the properties of the Form using the following information:<ul><li>Size: **600, 300**</li><li>Text: **Order Details**</li></ul></li></ul>
3. Add a data source to the application.	<ul><li>See the resource in the Lab Toolkit, *Using a Web Service Data Source.*</li><li>Run the Data Source Configuration Wizard to add the data source to the project using the following information:<ul><li>Data source type: **Web Service**</li><li>Web reference: Use the URL **http://london/OrdersWebService/Service.asmx**</li></ul></li></ul>

(continued)

Tasks	Supporting information
4. Drag the **OrdersData** table onto the form.	See the resource in the Lab Toolkit, *Using a Web Service Data Source*. ■ From the Data Sources window, drag the **OrdersData** table onto the form. • Notice that the drop-down list for the **OrdersData** table in the Data Sources window allows you to select **Details** layout, but Visual Studio 2005 does not allow you to drop the table onto the form while Details layout is selected. • Notice also that when you drop the table in Grid layout onto the form, Visual Studio 2005 generates a BindingNavigator at the top of the form. A BindingNavigator is usually used with Details layout, not Grid layout. This is incorrect behavior in Visual Studio 2005 Beta 2 and should be fixed in a future release. ■ Delete the **OrdersDataBindingNavigator** control from the top of the form. This is not required in Grid layout. ■ Click the **SmartTag** for **OrdersDataDataGridView**. Open the drop-down list for **Choose Data Source**. • Notice that the **OrdersDataDataGridView** control is currently bound to **OrdersDataBindingSource**. This is incorrect—a limitation of Visual Studio 2005 Beta 2. • Expand **OrdersDataBindingSource** and select the **Order Details** table instead. • Clear **Enable Adding**, **Enable Editing** and **Enable Deleting**.
5. Design the form.	■ View Form1 in the designer window and then add a **Button** control. ■ Set the properties of the **Button** control using the following information: • (Name): **GetDataButton** • Location: **0, 0** • Text: **Get Data** ■ Set the properties of the **OrdersDataDataGridView** control using the following information: • Location: **0, 30** • Size: **591, 247**

(continued)

Tasks	Supporting information

6. Write code for the form.	See the resource in the Lab Toolkit, *Using a Web Service Data Source*.
	
	■ View the code window for **Form1** and add code to do the following:
	
	   • Declare an instance variable and name it **ordersService** of type **London.Service**.
	
	```csharp\n//C#\nprivate london.Service ordersService;\n```
	```vbnet\n'Visual Basic\nPrivate ordersService As london.Service\n```
	   • In the **Form_Load** event, instantiate this variable, setting it to a new instance of the **london.Service** class.
	
	```csharp\n//C#\nordersService = new london.Service();\n```
	```vbnet\n'Visual Basic\nordersService = New london.Service()\n```
	   • **Visual Basic projects only**: Add an **Imports** statement for the **System.Data** namespace.
	
	   • In the **GetDataButton_Click** event, declare an **OrdersClient.london.OrdersData** variable and set it to the return value from the **GetDataSet** method of the **ordersService** object. Set the **DataSource** property of the **ordersDataBindingSource** object to the **OrdersData** DataSet you just created.
	
	```csharp\n//C#\nOrdersClient.london.OrdersData OrdersData;\nOrdersData = ordersService.GetDataSet();\nordersDataBindingSource.DataSource = OrdersData;\n```
	```vbnet\n'Visual Basic\nDim OrdersData As OrdersClient.london.OrdersData\nOrdersData = ordersService.GetDataSet()\nOrdersDataBindingSource.DataSource = OrdersData\n```

7. Build and test the application.	■ Set the **OrdersClient** project as a startup project. ■ Build the application and resolve any compile errors. ■ Run the application and verify that the **Get Data** button populates the grid with the order details data.

Exercise 3
Implementing Asynchronous Calls to a Web Service Data Source

In this exercise, you will modify the Windows Form application to enable users to cancel long-running data requests.

Scenario

Users may be running this application over a slow Internet connection. Therefore, the ability to cancel a long-running data request is required. You will change the application to call the Web service asynchronously and add functionality to cancel a request.

Tasks	Supporting information
1. Add a button to the form.	▪ Add another **Button** control to the Windows Form, and set its properties using the following information: • (Name): **CancelAsyncButton** • Enabled: **False** • Location: **82, 0** • Text: **Cancel**

2. Write code to invoke the Web service asynchronously.	See the resource in the Lab Toolkit, *Asynchronous Calls Using Data Source*.
	
	▪ View the code window for Form1 and add code to do the following:
	• Declare an instance variable named **token** of type **object**.
	• In the **Form1_Load** event, link the **ordersService GetDataSetCompleted** event to a method named **GetDataSetCompleted** that you will write later, as shown in the following code:
	
	`//C#`
	`ordersService.GetDataSetCompleted += new`
	`  london.GetDataSetCompletedEventHandler(this.GetData`
	`SetCompleted);`
	
	`'Visual Basic`
	`AddHandler ordersService.GetDataSetCompleted,`
	`AddressOf GetDataSetCompleted`
	
	• In the **Form1_Load** event, instantiate the *token* variable as an array of objects and assign the first member the value **1**.
	• Delete the code in the **GetDataButton_Click** event, and replace it with code to call the **GetDataSetAsync** method of the **ordersService** object, passing the token variable as its parameter, and then enable the **CancelAsyncButton** control.
	• In the **CancelAsyncButton_Click** event, call the **CancelAsync** method of the **ordersService** object, passing the token variable.

(*continued*)

Tasks	Supporting information
2. (*continued*)	• Add a new method and name it **GetDataSetCompleted**, as shown in the following code: ```//C#\nvoid GetDataSetCompleted(object sender,\n london.GetDataSetCompletedEventArgs args)\n\n'Visual Basic\nSub GetDataSetCompleted(ByVal sender As Object, _\n ByVal args As london.GetDataSetCompletedEventArgs)\n\nEnd Sub``` • Add code to the method to test whether the **GetDataSet** method call was canceled. If so, display a message box informing the user that the method was canceled; if not, set the **DataSource** property of the **OrdersDataBindingSource** to **the Order_Details** table returned in the **args.Result** object, and also disable the **CancelAsyncButton**.

3. Build and test the application.	▪ Build the application and resolve any compile errors.
	▪ Run the application and verify the following:
	    • If you click **Get Data** and then immediately click **Cancel**, the call is canceled and you are informed of the cancellation.
	    • If you click **Get Data** and allow the call to complete, the grid is populated with the order details data.

Lab 4C: Publishing Using ClickOnce

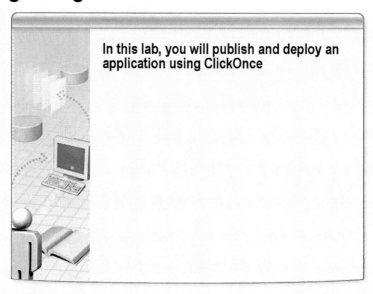

In this lab, you will publish and deploy an application using ClickOnce

After completing this lab, you will be able to:

- Deploy a Windows Forms application to a Web Server.
- Install an application to a remote client.
- Write an application that automatically updates when a new version is deployed.

 Important You can choose to program with either Visual C# or Visual Basic in this workshop. Code samples and lab solutions are provided in both programming languages. If you prefer, you can choose to perform some labs using one programming language, and perform others using the other language. However, once you start a lab, you should complete all lab exercises using the same programming language.

Lab Setup

For this lab, you will use the LONDON Virtual PC.

To prepare for this lab:

1. If LONDON is still running after the previous lab, on the **Action** menu, click **Close**. The **Action** menu is visible when the Virtual PC is running in windowed mode, but not when it is running full-screen. If you are running the Virtual PC full-screen, press <RIGHT>ALT+ENTER to switch to windowed mode.

2. In the **Close** window, select **Turn off and delete changes** and then click **OK**.

3. Start the LONDON Virtual PC. Do not use the LONDON UNIT 1 Virtual PC.

4. Log on as **Student** with a password of **Pa$$w0rd**.

5. Click the **Labfiles** Toolbar at the bottom right of the screen, and navigate to **Lab04c\Setup**.

6. Click the file **Install** to set up the Virtual PC for this lab. This script installs the starter code for this lab into Microsoft Visual SourceSafe®.

7. Enter the Administrator's password when prompted, which is **Pa$$w0rd**.

8. Press any key to exit the setup command procedure.

 Caution The setup procedure for this lab performs operations with the SQL Server. If you have recently started the virtual PC, the database server may not have completed its startup. If you run the install script and you see either of the following errors, wait a few minutes and then try to run the install script again:

- Client unable to establish connection
- Shared Memory Provider: The system cannot find the file specified.
- Timeout expired.

Lab Toolkit Resources

Use the following Lab Toolkit resources to help you complete this lab:

- ClickOnce Overview
- Designing ClickOnce Applications

Estimated time to complete this lab: **45 minutes**

Lab Solution Files

There are Visual Basic and Visual C# solution files associated with the labs in this workshop. The lab solution files are located in the folder E:\Microsoft Learning\2364\Labfiles\Lab04c\Solution on the Virtual PC.

Exercise 1
Preparing for ClickOnce application publishing

In this exercise you will prepare a Web server so that the development team can publish a Windows Forms application using Visual Studio 2005.

Scenario

Northwind Traders requires applications to be deployed to employees in a secure and available manner. Northwind Traders wants to ensure that applications can be installed from an intranet site. The Web server administration team needs to prepare a staging server so that the development team can publish ClickOnce applications to the staging site.

The development team has been notified by the server administrators that the staging server has been configured for ClickOnce deployment. You have been asked by the team leader to publish the OrdersClient application.

Tasks	Supporting information
1. Start Visual Studio 2005 using the **Administrator** account.	▪ To use ClickOnce publishing in Visual Studio 2005, you must be a member of the Administrators group. The **Student** account is not an administrator but is only in the Users group. ▪ From the **Start** menu, point to All Programs, point to **Microsoft Visual Studio 2005 Beta 2**, right-click **Microsoft Visual Studio 2005 Beta 2**, and then click **Run as**. ▪ Click **The following user** and type **Administrator** for the user name, and **Pa$$w0rd** for the password. Click **OK**. ▪ **Additional Information** The Student account is a member of the Users security group. The ClickOnce application deployment process will create a virtual directory to be created on the staging server. IIS requires that the virtual directory be created by an account with administrative privileges. ▪ As we are using Windows XP, we will run Visual Studio 2005 as the Administrator for this unit. On server operating systems, such as Windows Server 2003, there is the possibility of using Web Operator privileges to create virtual directories. Windows XP uses Peer Web Services and there is no facility for separate Web Operators. ▪ When Visual Studio 2005 starts, the **Choose Default Environment Settings** dialog box may be displayed if this is the first time that the **Administrator** has started it. Choose the settings appropriate for the language you are using (Visual Basic or Visual C#), and then click **Start Visual Studio**.

(continued)

Tasks	Supporting information
2. Open either the Visual Basic or Visual C# NorthwindSuppliers solution.	■ On the **File** menu, point to **Open**, and then click **Project/Solution**. ■ Click the **My SourceSafe(LAN)** icon. ■ Click the **SourceSafeDB** database and then click **Open**. ■ In the **Log on to Visual SourceSafe Database** dialog box, type the user name **Student**, leave the password blank, and then click **OK**. ■ Open the OrdersClient.sln file from 2364\Lab04c\VB\OrdersClient if you are going to complete the lab using Visual Basic. ■ If you are going to complete the lab using Visual C#, open the OrdersClient.sln file from 2364\Lab04c\CS\OrdersClient. **Additional Information** The solution may take a little time to load. The projects will be retrieved as a background task and you can carry on working, but you will not be able to build the application until the solution has been completely retrieved.
3. Build and test the project.	■ Build the **OrdersClient** solution. ■ Run the application to view suppliers orders. ■ Close the application. You are now ready to publish it.
4. Configure the **ClickOnce Publishing** settings for the OrdersClient project and make the application ready for publishing.	See the resource in the Lab Toolkit, *ClickOnce Overview*. ■ Display the **Properties** page for the **OrdersClient** project and click the **Publish** tab. ■ If necessary, change the Publishing Location to **http://localhost/OrdersClient**. ■ Under **Install Mode and Settings**, confirm **The application is available offline as well (launchable from Start menu)** is selected. ■ Ensure that the **Publish Version** is set to **1.0.0.0** and that **Automatically increment revision with each publish** is selected.
5. Review the Application Files necessary to remotely install the application.	■ Click the **Application Files** button. ■ In the **Application Files** dialog box, ensure that the OrdersClient.exe file is marked as **Required**. Click **OK**. **Note** In certain cases, such as an XSD file, you may need to set a file's build action property as Content in order for it to appear in the Application Files list so it may be set as Required for publication.
6. Explore the Prerequisites necessary to run the application on a remote client.	■ Click the **Prerequisites** button. ■ Ensure that the **.NET Framework 2.0 Beta** is selected as a prerequisite. Click **OK**.

(*continued*)

Tasks	Supporting information
7. View the Application Updates settings.	■ Click the **Updates** button. ■ In the **Application Updates** dialog box, ensure that **The application should check for updates** is selected. ■ For the **Choose when the application should check for updates** option, confirm **Before the application starts** is selected. ■ Click **OK**.
8. Examine the publish options.	■ Click the **Options** button. ■ In the **Publish Options** dialog box, ensure that **Publish language** is set to **(Default)**. ■ Confirm **Automatically generate deployment web page after every publish** and **Open deployment web page after publish** are selected. If it does not exist, it will be created. Set the Deployment web page to **publish.htm**. Click **OK**.
9. Publish the application using the Publish Wizard.	See the resource in the Lab Toolkit, *ClickOnce Overview*. ■ Click the **Publish Wizard** button. ■ In the **Where do you want to publish the application?** Page of the wizard, type **http://localhost/OrdersClient** if necessary. Click **Next**. ■ In the **Will the application be available offline?** page, confirm **Yes, this application is available online or offline** is selected. Click **Next**. ■ In the **Ready to Publish** page, click **Finish**. ■ Watch the status bar at the bottom of the Visual Studio 2005 window. You will see publishing messages appear. More detailed messages appear in the Output window. If you cannot see the Output window, on the **View** menu, click **Other Windows**, and then click **Output**. **Tip** If the Welcome to the New Connection Wizard page appears, click Cancel, and then click the Publish Wizard button again. This page appears because the Virtual PC you are using does not have an Internet connection and is due to the process used to generate the key file. On the subsequent run, the key file will have been created and the process completes as expected.

(*continued*)

Tasks	Supporting information
10. View publish.htm with Internet Explorer. Do *not* install the application at this stage.	▪ Once your application has been successfully published, Internet Explorer will automatically display publish.htm with a link allowing you to install the application and another link to the ClickOnce Help site on MSDN. ▪ Do *not* click on the link to install the application. Application installation is covered in the next exercise. ▪ Close Internet Explorer.
11. Explore the Web site that has been created on the local Web server ready for ClickOnce application installation.	▪ Using Windows Explorer, browse to **C:\Inetpub\wwwroot\OrdersClient**. ▪ Examine the folder structure and files you find there. For example, view the file **OrdersClient_1_0_0_0\ OrdersClient.exe.manifest** using Notepad. ▪ Close Windows Explorer. See the resource in the Lab Toolkit, *ClickOnce Overview*.

Exercise 2
Installing the OrdersClient Application

In this exercise, you will deploy the ClickOnce application.

Scenario

Having published the application, the Northwind developers want to verify that the ClickOnce application deployment process operates as expected on a local system.

Tasks	Supporting information
1. Open the **Add or Remove Programs** application from Control Panel to verify that the OrdersClient application is not currently installed.	■ On the **Start** menu, click **Control Panel**. ■ Double-click **Add or Remove Programs**. ■ Review the currently installed programs; note the OrdersClient application is not installed. ■ Close the **Add or Remove Programs** dialog box. Close Control Panel.
2. Open Internet Explorer and browse to the URL, http://london/OrdersClient/publish.htm.	■ Open Internet Explorer and open the URL http://london/OrdersClient/publish.htm. **Note** LONDON already has the prerequisite .NET Framework 2.0 installed. The link will install only the application, and the text below the link confirms this.
3. Install the OrdersClient application.	■ In the OrdersClient window, click **Install**. ■ A warning dialog box states that the publisher of the application cannot be verified. Although it is possible to set yourself up as a trusted source, this feature is not explored in this workshop. ■ In the application warning dialog box, click **More Information** and then notice the security issues identified by the installer. ■ Continue the installation. Close the warning notice and then click **Install**. The OrdersClient application is installed and started automatically. ■ Verify that the OrdersClient application operates as expected, and then close the application. ■ Close the Internet Explorer window displaying publish.htm.
4. Return to Control panel and open the **Add or Remove Programs** dialog box.	■ Open Control Panel and double-click the **Add or Remove Programs** icon. ■ Review the currently installed programs; note that the OrdersClient program is now an installed application. ■ Close the **Add or Remove Programs** dialog box and close Control Panel.

(*continued*)

Tasks	Supporting information
5. Run the newly installed application from the Start menu.	▪ From the **Start** menu, point to **All Programs**, point to the **Northwind Traders** Program Group, and then run the **OrdersClient** application. ▪ Verify that the application starts, and then close it.
6. Save the OrdersClient application.	▪ Save the project in Visual Studio 2005 by clicking the **Save All** button. ▪ Leave the project open in Visual Studio 2005. You will come back to it in Exercise 4.

Exercise 3
Installing the OrdersClient Application on a Remote Client

In this exercise, you will install the OrdersClient application on a remote client.

Scenario

Having published the application, the Northwind developers want to test the ClickOnce application deployment on a client system.

Tasks	Supporting information
1. Log on to the DENVER Virtual PC with the **Student** account and a password of **Pa$$w0rd**. Leave the LONDON Virtual PC running.	**Note** If you are in full-screen mode, press <RIGHT>ALT+ENTER to swap back to the host computer operating system. ■ Open the Virtual PC Console on the host computer. ■ Select the DENVER Virtual PC and click the **Start** button. ■ Log on to the Virtual PC with the **Student** account and a password of **Pa$$w0rd**.
2. On the DENVER Virtual PC, open Internet Explorer. Browse to the publish.htm page on the LONDON Web server.	■ Open Internet Explorer from the Start menu. ■ In the address bar type **http://london/OrdersClient/publish.htm**. ■ Click the **Go** button. ■ The OrdersClient application installation page is displayed. **Note** The .NET Framework version 2.0 has already been installed on DENVER. However, when deploying to a remote client that does not have .NET Framework 2.0 installed, then the account used on the remote client must have administrative privileges. That requirement applies only to the initial installation. Thereafter, an ordinary user account can be used to install and run ClickOnce applications.
3. Install and test the OrdersClient application.	■ In the OrdersClient window, click **Install**. ■ The OrdersClient application installation page is displayed. ■ A security warning dialog warns that the publisher of the application cannot be verified. Although it is possible to set up your organization as a trusted source, we have not explored that feature in this workshop. ■ Click **Install** in the **Application Install - Security Warning** dialog box. ■ The OrdersClient application is installed and started automatically. ■ Verify that the OrdersClient application operates as expected.
4. Shut down the DENVER Virtual PC.	■ Close the OrdersClient application. ■ Close the Internet Explorer window displaying publish.htm. ■ Shut down the DENVER Virtual PC. Select Turn off and delete changes.

Exercise 4
Updating an Application Using ClickOnce

In this exercise, you will update the OrdersClient application and test the Automatic Update feature of ClickOnce.

Scenario

Having published the application, the Northwind developers want to add further visual information to the application and redeploy this new version of the application using ClickOnce. You will test the application updates correctly on the local LONDON Virtual PC.

Tasks	Supporting information
1. Return to the LONDON Virtual PC editing the OrdersClient application you were working on in Exercise 3.	■ Return to Visual Studio 2005 on the LONDON Virtual PC. The OrdersClient solution should still be open. 💡 **Tip** If you closed Visual Studio 2005 during the earlier exercise, use the following steps to reopen the OrdersClient solution: ■ Start Visual Studio 2005 using **Run As** and the **Administrator** account, in the same way as you did in Exercise 1. ■ Open the OrdersClient application using Microsoft Visual SourceSafe from 2364\Lab04c\VB\OrdersClient if you are completing the lab with Visual Basic. ■ If you are completing the lab with Visual C#, open your project with Visual SourceSafe from 2364\Lab04c\CS\OrdersClient.
2. Open the Form1.cs or Form1.vb Designer.	■ Open Form1.vb in Designer view if you are performing the lab using Visual Basic. ■ Open Form1.cs in Designer view if you are performing the lab using Visual C#.
3. Amend the **Text** property of the Suppliers form to read **Order Details Query**.	■ In the **View** menu, click **Properties Window**. ■ Select the **Form1** object in the Designer. ■ Change the **Text** property to read **Order Details Query**.
4. Build the application.	■ Build the solution and correct any errors.
5. Republish the application.	■ Open the Properties page of the OrdersClient project. ■ Click the **Publish** tab. ■ Check that the **Revision** has incremented automatically. (If the revision has not incremented, close the Properties page, click the **Save All** button, and then redisplay the Properties page. If the increment still does not update, change the Revision number manually.) ■ Click the **Publish Wizard** button. Accept the default settings at each step and click **Finish**. ■ When the application has published successfully, **publish.htm** will be displayed in Internet Explorer. ■ Close the browser window. You will *not* need to reinstall the application in this way.

(continued)

Tasks	Supporting information
6. Explore the new installation files that have been created on the LONDON Web server.	▪ Using Windows Explorer, browse to the C:\Inetpub\wwwroot\OrdersClient folder. ▪ You will notice a new subfolder containing all the files necessary to update existing applications, OrdersClient_1_0_0_1. ▪ Close Windows Explorer.
7. Test the automatic update feature of ClickOnce.	▪ From the **Start** menu, point to **All Programs**, point to the **Northwind Traders** program group, and then click **OrdersClient**.
8. Install updates to the application and test the application to ensure that it works correctly.	▪ The system checks to see if any updates to your application are required and then the **Update Available** dialog box appears. ▪ Click **OK** to download the update. Notice that the user has the option to skip the update. ▪ The update progresses and the OrdersClient application automatically starts. ▪ Verify that the application still works as expected and that the application's title bar has changed.
9. Close the application.	▪ Close the OrdersClient application.
10. Save and close your Visual Studio 2005 solution.	▪ In Visual Studio 2005, check the changes made to the solution into Visual SourceSafe by clicking the **Check In** button from the Pending Checkins window. ▪ Save the files and, from the **File** menu, click **Close Solution**.

Lab Discussion

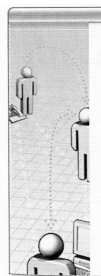

- • How will the use of data sources simplify your development activities?
- • How will the DataSet Designer simplify your development activities?
- • Which of the new controls will be of most benefit to you?
- • How will the use of different types of data sources enhance your data-oriented applications?
- • What are the advantages and disadvantages of using the generated data sources in middle-tier components?
- • What uses do you have for Web service data sources?

In Lab 4A, you have used many of the new Windows Forms features provided by the .NET Framework 2.0 and built a Windows Forms application using the new RAD data binding features provided by Visual Studio 2005.

- ■ How will the use of data sources simplify the development of your data-oriented applications?

- ■ Share your experiences creating typed **DataSet** classes, and discuss how the new **DataSet Designer** will simplify future efforts.

- ■ Discuss with the class the new controls you have used and whether you see yourself using them in future applications. Will any of the new controls provide a replacement for a third-party or custom control you are currently using?

In lab 4B, you have learned how to build multitier data-bound applications, using both object and Web service data sources.

- ■ How will the use of different types of data sources enhance your data-oriented applications?

- ■ What are the advantages and disadvantages of using the generated data sources in middle-tier components?

- ■ Discuss with the class ideas you may have for using Web service data sources in your future applications.

Lab Discussion (*continued*)

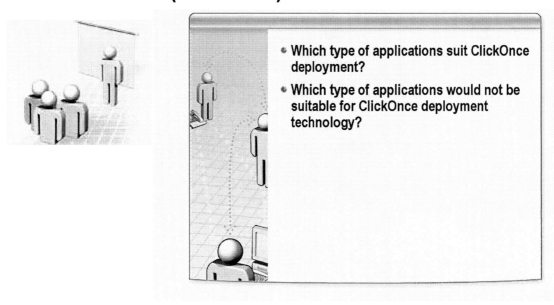

* Which type of applications suit ClickOnce deployment?
* Which type of applications would not be suitable for ClickOnce deployment technology?

In Lab 4C, you have learned how to use the new ClickOnce publishing wizards in Visual Studio 2005.

- Discuss with the class the advantages ClickOnce application deployment provides for developing applications in your workplace.

- Discuss with the class the application architecture scenarios suitable to take advantage of ClickOnce.

Unit 5: Building Presentation-Layer Applications with ASP.NET 2.0

Contents

Information in this document, including URL and other Internet Web site references, is subject to change without notice. Unless otherwise noted, the example companies, organizations, products, domain names, e-mail addresses, logos, people, places, and events depicted herein are fictitious, and no association with any real company, organization, product, domain name, e-mail address, logo, person, place or event is intended or should be inferred. Complying with all applicable copyright laws is the responsibility of the user. Without limiting the rights under copyright, no part of this document may be reproduced, stored in or introduced into a retrieval system, or transmitted in any form or by any means (electronic, mechanical, photocopying, recording, or otherwise), or for any purpose, without the express written permission of Microsoft Corporation.

The names of manufacturers, products, or URLs are provided for informational purposes only and Microsoft makes no representations and warranties, either expressed, implied, or statutory, regarding these manufacturers or the use of the products with any Microsoft technologies. The inclusion of a manufacturer or product does not imply endorsement of Microsoft of the manufacturer or product. Links are provided to third party sites. Such sites are not under the control of Microsoft and Microsoft is not responsible for the contents of any linked site or any link contained in a linked site, or any changes or updates to such sites. Microsoft is not responsible for webcasting or any other form of transmission received from any linked site. Microsoft is providing these links to you only as a convenience, and the inclusion of any link does not imply endorsement of Microsoft of the site or the products contained therein.

Microsoft may have patents, patent applications, trademarks, copyrights, or other intellectual property rights covering subject matter in this document. Except as expressly provided in any written license agreement from Microsoft, the furnishing of this document does not give you any license to these patents, trademarks, copyrights, or other intellectual property.

© 2005 Microsoft Corporation. All rights reserved.

Microsoft, ActiveX, IntelliSense, MSDN, MS-DOS, PowerPoint, Visual Basic, Visual C#, Visual SourceSafe, Visual Studio, Visual Web Developer, Windows, Windows Media, Windows NT, and Windows Server are either registered trademarks or trademarks of Microsoft Corporation in the United States and/or other countries.

All other trademarks are property of their respective owners.

Overview

- Data Source Controls
- Retrieving Relational Data
- Data Binding with Relational Data
- Retrieving XML Data
- Demonstration: RAD Data Binding in ASP.NET 2.0
- Master Pages
- Site Navigation
- Themes
- Membership and Role Management
- ASP.NET Web Site Administration Tool
- Lab 5A: RAD Data Binding in ASP.NET 2.0
- Lab 5B: Programming Master Pages, Site Navigation, and Themes
- Lab 5C: Membership and Role Management in ASP.NET 2.0
- Lab Discussion

Most Web applications display data of one sort or another. In this unit, you will learn how to use some of the new features in ASP.NET 2.0 to build data-bound applications rapidly.

You will also learn about three major new enhancements that simplify the creation and maintenance of structured, consistent, and navigable Web applications: master pages, site navigation, and themes.

These features, which previously would have been implemented as custom solutions or by using third-party products, now form part of the standard ASP.NET framework and can be implemented rapidly in new or existing Web applications by using Microsoft® Visual Studio® 2005.

In the final part of this module, you will learn about the features in ASP.NET 2.0 for managing Web site membership and role membership. One of the primary goals of the ASP.NET 2.0 release is to provide easy ways to implement commonly used functionality and to reduce manual and repetitive coding for ASP.NET developers. The membership controls are a good example of new functionality that has been added to the ASP.NET product that help to achieve this goal.

Objectives

After completing this unit, you will be able to:

- Describe the new data source controls: **SqlDataSource**, **ObjectDataSource**, **AccessDataSource**, **SiteMapDataSource**, and **XmlDataSource**.

- Perform data binding to relational data in an ASP.NET application by using the **SqlDataSource** control.

- Perform common data-handling operations, such as sorting, paging, updating, inserting, and deleting, by using the **GridView** control.

- Create Web Forms that display Master-Details data relationships with little or no code by using the **DetailsView** control.

- Perform data binding to Extensible Markup Language (XML) data in an ASP.NET application by using the **XmlDataSource** control.

- Apply a consistent page layout across a Web application by using master pages.

- Create highly navigable Web applications by using site navigation.

- Implement a consistent and easily maintainable appearance or Web applications by using themes.

- Manage users by using the Login controls.

- Manage user credentials and role groups.

- Manage a Web site by using the ASP.NET Web Site Administration Tool.

Data Source Controls

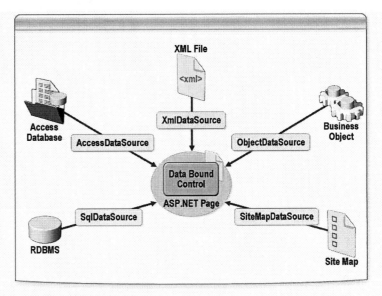

When you need to access data in an ASP.NET application, you can use a data source control to encapsulate the connection and command information necessary to retrieve, and even update, the data. This control-based approach to retrieving data makes it possible to build data-centric Web applications with minimal coding effort.

ASP.NET 2.0 includes five data source controls, each designed to access a specific kind of data store, as described in the following table:

Data Source Control	Description
SqlDataSource	Use the **SqlDataSource** control to access data in a relational database management system (RDBMS) such as Microsoft SQL Server™. The **SqlDataSource** control works with providers for SQL Server (version 7.0 or later,) Oracle, Open Database Connectivity (ODBC) data sources, and object linking and embedding database (OLE DB) data sources.
AccessDataSource	The **AccessDataSource** control is designed for accessing Microsoft JET database files (.mdb files), such as those created using Microsoft Office Access. Although you can also connect to Access databases by using an OLE DB provider with the **SqlDataSource** control, the **AccessDataSource** control provides a simpler programming model in which the **DataFile** property can be used to reference the database file instead of a full-connection string.
XmlDataSource	Use the **XmlDataSource** control to access data in an XML file. You can also specify an XML schema to return data-type information, an XML Stylesheet Language Transformation (XSLT) to transform the data as it is retrieved, and an XPath expression that can be used to filter the data. Use this control when you want to bind hierarchical XML data.

*(**continued**)*

Data Source Control	Description
ObjectDataSource	You can use the **ObjectDataSource** control to retrieve data from a data component or custom business object. The object (which can also be a Web service proxy), must provide a method that returns data as an object that implements the **IEnumerable** interface (such as a DataSet), and methods to perform Insert, Update, and Delete functions.
SiteMapDataSource	The **SiteMapDataSource** is used to retrieve data from a site map provider (such as an **XmlSiteMapProvider** object). The **SiteMapDataSource** control can be used to implement site navigation using data-bound controls such as a **TreeList** control.

Retrieving Relational Data

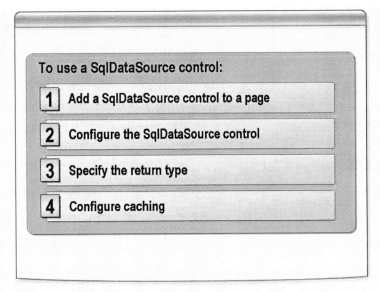

In most medium- to large-scale Web applications, you will retrieve relational data from a relational database management system such as Microsoft SQL Server. You can perform the following tasks with a **SqlDataSource** control in Visual Studio to retrieve relational data:

1. *Add a* **SqlDataSource** *control to a page.* The **SqlDataSource** control is used to map a set of data to a data-bound control. It encapsulates a connection to the data source and the commands used to retrieve, modify, insert, and delete data.

2. *Configure the* **SqlDataSource** *control.* The **SqlDataSource** control's smart tag can be used to specify the connection and command settings for the data source.

3. *Specify the return type.* You can choose to return data from the **SqlDataSource** control as a **DataSet** or a **DataReader**, depending on your needs.

4. *Configure caching.* You can use the **SqlDataSource** control's properties to configure data caching and improve performance.

Data Binding with Relational Data

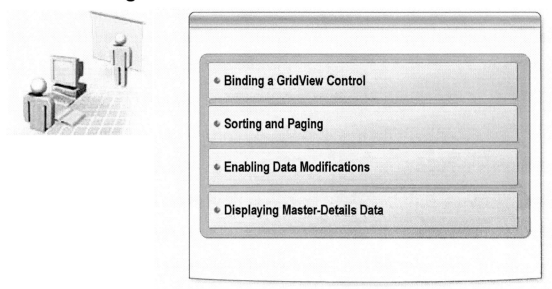

- Binding a GridView Control

- Sorting and Paging

- Enabling Data Modifications

- Displaying Master-Details Data

A number of data-bound controls can be used with one of the data source controls to display relational data. One of the more versatile of these is the **GridView** control, which is used to display data in a tabular format.

Binding a GridView Control

When you create a **SqlDataSource** control by dragging a table to a page, a **GridView** control is automatically created and bound to the **SqlDataSource**. Alternatively, you can drag a **GridView** control from the **Data** section of the Toolbox and set its **DataSource** property to an existing **SqlDataSource** control.

By default, the **GridView** control will automatically generate the columns required for the data returned by the **SqlDataSource**. If you want to control how the columns are displayed or if you want to add additional columns, you can configure them explicitly through the **Columns** property or by selecting **Edit Column** in the control's smart tag.

Sorting and Paging

You can enable sorting and paging when the **SqlDataSource** returns a **DataSet**. To enable sorting, set the **GridView** control's **AllowSorting** property to **True**; to enable paging, set the **AllowPaging** property to **True**. These properties can also be set through the **GridView** control's smart tag.

When sorting is enabled, users can sort the data by clicking a column heading. When paging is enabled, the **GridView** displays data in pages, the size of which is specified by the **PageSize** property. Users can click navigation links at the bottom of the grid to move between the pages. The format of the navigation controls is determined by the **Mode** property of the **GridView** control's **PagerSettings** property; the default value for this property is numeric, which results in a numeric link for each page.

Enabling Data Modifications

If the **SqlDataSource** control has been configured with appropriate **Update**, **Insert**, and **Delete** commands, the **GridView** control can be used to edit and update data. To enable data modifications through the **GridView** control, select **Enable Inserting**, **Enable Editing**, and **Enable Deleting** in the control's smart tag as required.

Displaying Master-Details Data

In many cases, you will want to display detail data based on a selection the user has made. For example, you might want to display a list of product categories, and then display the products in the category that the user selects.

You can use any data-bound control to display details, but the **DetailsView** control is specifically designed with this scenario in mind. Typically, you will display your master data in a **GridView**, and display details data in a **DetailsView** when the user selects a row in the **GridView**.

Retrieving XML Data

Retrieving XML Data with an XmlDataSource Control:

- DataFile: The XML file containing the data
- SchemaFile: An XML schema for the data
- TransformFile: An XSLT stylesheet
- XPath: An XPath expression to filter the data

Binding XML Data to a TreeView Control:

- Create explicit node bindings
- Set TextField and ValueField properties

Many applications exchange data using XML. In some scenarios, you might want to retrieve data from an XML file and display it on an ASP.NET page. You can use the **XmlDataSource** control to retrieve data from an XML file, and bind it to an XML-aware control, such as a **TreeView** control.

To implement data binding with XML using an **XmlDataDource** and a **TreeView**, you must perform the following steps:

1. Add an **XmlDataSource** and a **TreeView** to the page. You can drag these controls from the Toolbox, or drag an XML file from Solution Explorer onto the page (which will automatically create the required controls).

2. Configure the **XmlDataSource** to retrieve data from an XML file. You can optionally choose to associate an XML schema with the file to provide data type information. You can also apply an XSLT style sheet to transform the data, and specify an XPath expression to filter the data.

3. Configure the node bindings in the **TreeView** control to display the appropriate values from the XML file.

Demonstration: RAD Data Binding in ASP.NET 2.0

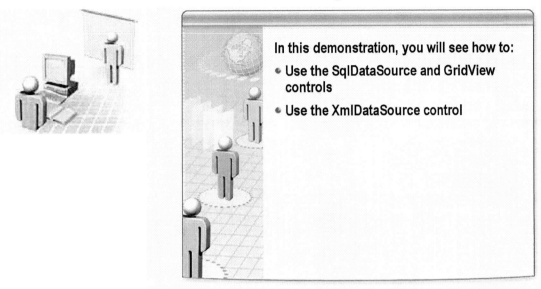

In this demonstration, you will see how to implement data binding in ASP.NET 2.0.

Master Pages

* **Master pages:**
  * Use the new @master directive
  * Specify standard page layout and content for a set of content pages
  * Contain named regions (content placeholders) where content pages can display custom content
* **Content pages:**
  * Identify a single master page using the MasterPageFile attribute of the @page directive
  * Implement content to fill content placeholders specified in master
  * Provide programmatic access to the controls and public members of their master page
* **Nested master pages enable the creation of page hierarchies to modularize standard layout and content**
* **Visual Studio 2005 supports the creation and graphical editing of master and content pages**

Users expect Web applications to be functional and easy to use. The layout of pages and the visual appearance of content and controls are important for branding and corporate image, but also contribute significantly to the experience users have when they use a Web application. Unfortunately, as Web applications grow, maintaining a consistent layout and appearance across the entire application becomes increasingly difficult and expensive. This is especially true when many people (or even teams) contribute to the overall application.

A master page sets the standard layout and content that you want to appear in a set of content pages. In addition, a master page includes named regions (or content placeholders) for which content pages can provide custom content. A content page is a simplified .aspx file that identifies only its master page and the content necessary to fill the content placeholders specified in the master.

When a user requests a content page by its Uniform Resource Locator (URL) (users do not request master pages), ASP.NET 2.0 merges the requested content page with its master page and returns the combined content of the two pages to the user. The existence of master pages and the process of merging master and content pages are transparent to the user.

The relationship between master and content pages means that updating standard layout and content across all content pages is simply a matter of making the change to the single master page. This can dramatically reduce the time and cost of Web application maintenance.

Master Pages Architecture Summary

Here is a summary of the key features of the master page architecture:

- Common page architecture

  Master pages are standard ASP.NET pages that have an extension of .master instead of .aspx and have a **@master** directive in the page instead of a **@page** directive. Master pages can include anything that you would place in a normal .aspx page, but use **ContentPlaceHolder** controls to identify regions where content pages can display custom content.

- One master page for many content pages

  Any number of content pages can bind to a single master page to provide standard page layout and content. Each content page identifies its master in the **masterPageFile** attribute of its @page directive. A master page has no awareness of the content pages that reference it. This provides a scalable architecture suitable for even the largest Web application.

- Nested master pages

  A master page can bind to its own master page, which in turn can bind to another master page, and so on. Each nested master page provides content to fill the content placeholders of its master. This content can also include new content placeholders that content pages (or other nested master pages) can populate with custom content. This enables the creation of a master page hierarchy to modularize the standard layout and content of a Web application.

- Programmability

  Content pages can access the public properties and methods of their immediate master page through their **Master** property, which returns a **System.Web.UI.Page** instance representing the master page. Content pages can also access the controls of their master page based on control names using the **Master.FindControl** method.

Visual Studio 2005 Support for Master Pages

Visual Studio 2005 provides the following support for the creation of ASP.NET Web applications that use master pages:

- Create new master pages using the Master Page template in the **Add New Item** dialog box.

- Create new content pages by selecting the **Select master page** check box when you create a standard Web Form using the **Add New Item** dialog box.

- Create new content pages directly from an open master page by right-clicking and selecting **Add Content Page** on the shortcut menu. The newly created content page is configured to use the master page from which it was created.

- Edit the standard layout and content of a master page using both the Design and Source page views provided by Visual Studio 2005. The graphical editing of master pages includes full Toolbox drag-and-drop support.

- Edit the custom content of a content page using both the Design and Source page views. The graphical editing of content pages includes full drag-and-drop Toolbox support and provides a preview of the content inherited from the master page.

 Important Visual Studio 2005 does not support the graphic editing of nested master pages or of the content pages that use them. To edit such pages, it is necessary to code the page manually using Source view.

Site Navigation

* **Site Map**
    * Describes logical site structure
    * Stored in any type of data store for which a site map provider exists
* **Site Map Provider**
    * Follows "Provider Pattern" (must extend SiteMapProvider class)
    * Provides link between Site Map and SiteMap object model
    * XML provider uses Web.sitemap file (standard/default SiteMapDataProvider)
* **SiteMap object model (SiteMap and SiteMapNode classes)**
    * Uses replaceable provider to access Site Map data
    * Provides run-time access to navigation data for SiteMapPath and SiteMapDataSource controls, as well as custom controls and programs
* **SiteMapDataSource control provides bridge between SiteMap and standard data-bindable controls**
    * Tree controls – TreeView (new), Menu (new), ...
    * Flat controls – ListBox, BulletedListBox (new), ...

Another important factor in the usability of a Web application is its logical structure and the ability of users to effectively navigate through that structure. Primarily, users must understand where they are in the logical structure of large sites and must be able to jump quickly to the most important application pages.

All but the smallest Web application can become confusing for users if it does not provide appropriate navigational support. Principally, users need to be able to:

* Visualize the logical structure of a Web site.
* Access key application locations with as few clicks as possible.
* Understand where, in the logical site structure, they are at any time.
* Be able to move up easily to higher layers in the site hierarchy.

Most sites provide some form of navigation controls such as buttons or hyperlinks—often in their page headers or a side bar. Larger sites often provide a menu—usually in the form of a tree—that provides users greater flexibility to access key application functionality quickly. Another common feature is the breadcrumb, which shows users where they are in a site hierarchy, and provides links to jump to parent pages higher in the hierarchy. Figure 1 shows an example breadcrumb:

Northwind Home > Purchasing > Suppliers

Figure 1. Breadcrumb aids navigation on a Web page.

The set of enhancements collectively known as ASP.NET 2.0 site navigation provides all these capabilities and more. More importantly, site navigation is a standard part of the ASP.NET 2.0 Framework, is easy to implement in both new and existing applications, and is accessible to all Web applications using a simple and flexible programming model.

Site Navigation Architecture Summary

Here is a summary of the key features of the site navigation architecture:

- Site map

  Fundamental to site navigation is the site map, which provides a logical representation of a site for the purpose of navigation. The site map can be stored in any type of data store and in any format—a replaceable provider (a class that extends **SiteMapProvider**) provides higher-level site navigation elements with access to the site map data in a standardized format. An XML site map provider is included by default; it provides access to site map data stored in a file named Web.sitemap.

- Site Map object model

  A set of classes, including the **SiteMap** and **SiteMapNode**, provides standardized access to site map data, further abstracting the structure of the underlying site map data. The site map object model is used by the new **SiteMapPath** control and can be used by other custom controls as well as applications to access and manipulate site navigation data at run time.

- Data Source

  The **SiteMapDataSource** component provides an interface to the site map object model that allows any standard control that supports data binding to display site navigation data. The **SiteMapDataSource** component is configurable to support two broad categories of control: flat and tree. Flat controls, such as the **ListBox** and new **BulletedListBox** controls, show lists of items. Tree controls, such as the new **TreeView** and **Menu** controls, can show hierarchical data.

Visual Studio 2005 Support for ASP.NET Navigation

Visual Studio 2005 provides full support for implementing site navigation in new or existing applications. This support includes:

- Configuration using standard property pages, and drag-and-drop of site navigation controls.
- Configuration of data-bindable controls to use **SiteMapDataSource**.
- Display of static navigation data in data-bound controls in Design view.

Themes

- **Skin**
  - Collection of property values that define the visual appearance of a specific type of control e.g. Button, Calendar, or GridView
  - Defined using standard ASP.NET control syntax but with a reduced property set
- **Theme**
  - Named collection of skins, images, and style sheets
  - Specified at the page level using @page directive to apply appropriate skins and styles to all controls on the page
  - Specified at site or folder level using Web.config to affect all pages within scope
  - Programmable at run time to offer enhanced customization and personalization capabilities

Maintaining a consistent appearance and layout across all but the smallest Web applications is a significant challenge. Cascading Style Sheets (CSS) helps, but the scope of their configuration capabilities is limited when it comes to the controls in ASP.NET applications. Without using third-party tools or custom solutions, making changes to a Web application involves visiting each page and touching the necessary controls. This is a time-consuming, error-prone, and laborious process that requires discipline, and this process must be followed by extensive testing to get it right. ASP.NET 2.0 themes and skins provide a solution that is integrated with the ASP.NET framework; that integration dramatically simplifies the maintenance of Web applications.

Themes architecture summary

Here is a summary of the key features of the themes architecture:

- Skins

  A skin is a collection of property values that determine the visual appearance of a specific type of control, for example, the background and foreground colors of a **Button** control or the font type and size used in a **GridView** control.

- Themes

  A theme is a named collection of skins, images, and CSS values that can be applied to an entire Web application or a subset of the application's pages. Any controls contained in pages to which the theme applies will have the appropriate skins and styles applied to them before they are rendered. Theme-based properties override the properties set locally on the control unless theming is specifically turned off for the control by setting its **EnableTheming** property to **False**.

- Default and named skins

  A theme can contain only one default skin for each control type but can contain any number of named skins. An individual control can be configured to use a named skin by setting its **SkinID** property to the **ID** of the desired skin. Any control that does not specify a **SkinID** uses the default skin for that type of control.

- Maximize consistency and minimize maintenance

  By creating themes that contain consistent skins for all control types contained in an application, you can easily maintain a consistent appearance and layout across an entire application or a subset of pages. When you need to update the appearance of an application, you change the property values in a single location instead of visiting every page. Themes dramatically reduce the time and effort required to change the appearance of even the smallest Web site without the need to use external tools.

- Separation of responsibility

  Themes allow for true separation of the appearance and logic of an application. For the first time, it is realistically possible to give a design team total responsibility for the appearance of an application, while allowing the developers to focus on implementing its functionality.

- Simplify Customization and Personalization

  The ability to change active themes at run time provides new opportunities for customization and personalization support in Web applications.

Membership and Role Management

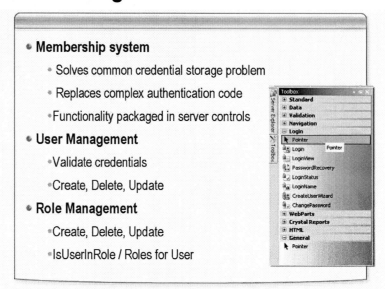

- Membership system
  - Solves common credential storage problem
  - Replaces complex authentication code
  - Functionality packaged in server controls
- User Management
  - Validate credentials
  - Create, Delete, Update
- Role Management
  - Create, Delete, Update
  - IsUserInRole / Roles for User

ASP.NET Membership

ASP.NET membership gives you a built-in way to validate and store user credentials. ASP.NET membership helps you manage user authentication in your Web sites. ASP.NET membership is ideal for implementing ASP.NET Forms authentication, where user credentials are entered through a dedicated page in your Web site. The **ASP.NET Login** controls are packaged server controls that make it extremely easy to create a complete system for authenticating users.

ASP.NET membership supports facilities for:

- Creating new users and passwords.

- Storing membership information (user names, passwords, and supporting data) in Microsoft SQL Server, Microsoft Access, or in an alternative data store.

- Authenticating users who visit your site. You can authenticate users programmatically, or you can use the **ASP.NET Login** controls to create a complete authentication system that requires little or no code.

- Managing passwords, which includes creating, changing, or resetting them, maintaining password expiration dates, and so on.

ASP.NET Role Management

ASP.NET role management lets you treat groups of users as a unit by assigning users to roles such as manager, sales, member, and so on. When you have assigned users to roles, you can limit access to creating resources in your Web site by specifying access rules in a Web.config file, or you can query role membership in code to limit access to resources.

For example, your site might include a set of pages that you want to display only to members. Similarly, you might want to show or hide a part of a page based on whether the current user is a manager. With roles, you can establish these types of rules independently of individual application users.

ASP.NET Web Site Administration Tool

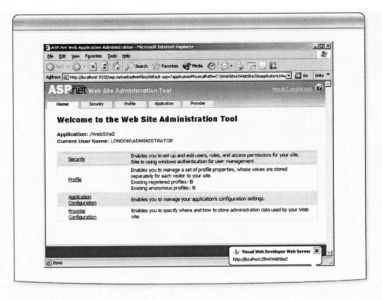

Much of the configuration of ASP.NET membership and ASP.NET role management is achieved by XML entries in the Web.config file for your application. You can edit this file manually, although for even moderately complex authentication and authorization systems, this can become a difficult and error-prone task.

ASP.NET 2.0 gives you an easy way to manage the settings contained in a Web.config file. You start the Web Site Administration Tool from the **Web site** menu in the Visual Studio 2005 IDE. This tool provides an easy way to manage:

- *Security settings.* The tool allows you to select between Microsoft Windows® or ASP.NET Forms authentication. You can also create, delete, and modify user details and roles, and you can assign users to roles.

- *Profile settings.* This sets profile properties that represent data specific to a particular user. Using profile properties enables you to dynamically customize your Web site for individual users.

- *Application configuration.* Here, you can specify application-specific data such as database connection strings, tracing, or site counters.

- *Provider configuration.* By default, the Web Site Administration Tool creates a Microsoft Access database to store many configuration settings. This section of the tool allows you to configure an alternative provider, such as a SQL Server database.

Lab 5A: RAD Data Binding with ASP.NET 2.0

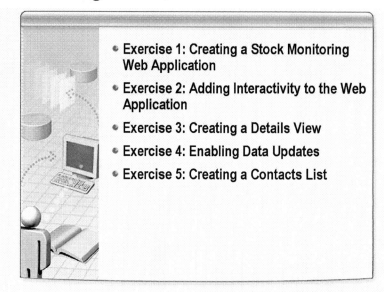

* Exercise 1: Creating a Stock Monitoring Web Application
* Exercise 2: Adding Interactivity to the Web Application
* Exercise 3: Creating a Details View
* Exercise 4: Enabling Data Updates
* Exercise 5: Creating a Contacts List

After completing this lab, you will be able to:

■ Perform data binding to relational data in an ASP.NET application by using the **SqlDataSource** control.

■ Perform common data-handling operations, such as sorting, paging, updating, inserting, and deleting, by using the **GridView** control.

■ Create Web Forms using little or no code that display Master-Details data relationships by using the **DetailsView** control.

■ Perform data binding to XML data in an ASP.NET application by using the **XmlDataSource** control.

Lab Setup

1. If the LONDON Virtual PC is still running after the previous lab, on the **Action** menu, click **Close**. The **Action** menu is visible when the Virtual PC is running in windowed mode, but not when it is running full-screen. If you are running the Virtual PC full-screen, press <RIGHT>ALT+ENTER to switch to windowed mode.

   In the Close window, select **Turn off and delete changes** and then click **OK**.

2. Start LONDON Virtual PC.

Lab Toolkit Resources

Use the following Lab Toolkit resources to help you complete this lab:

- Northwind Traders Technical Specification: Stock Level Monitoring Application
- Working with the **SqlDataSource** Control
- How to Implement Master-Detail Data Binding with the **GridView** and **DetailsView** Controls
- How to Implement Data-Bound Updates
- Data Binding with XML Data

Estimated time to complete this lab: **90 minutes**

Lab Solution Files

There are Microsoft Visual Basic® and Microsoft Visual C#® solution files associated with the labs in this workshop. The lab solution files are located in the folder E:\Microsoft Learning\2364\ Labfiles\Lab05a\Solution on the Virtual PCs.

Exercise 1
Creating a Stock Monitoring Web Application

In this exercise, you will develop an intranet application through which the management team at Northwind Traders can monitor stock levels. You will use a **SqlDataSource** control to retrieve data from a SQL Server database and bind it to **GridView** control on an ASP.NET page.

Scenario

As part of an ongoing project to automate Northwind Traders' stock management systems, you must develop a Web application through which the stock levels for each supplier can be monitored. In this first phase of the application development cycle, you must implement an application that lists the relevant details of each supplier.

Tasks	Supporting information
1. Log on to LONDON using the **Student** account.	▪ The current password for the Student account is **Pa$$w0rd**.
2. Read and understand the Program Design Specification.	See the Lab Toolkit resource, *Northwind Traders Technical Specification: Stock Level Monitoring Application*
3. Create a Web site, using the language of your choice.	▪ Open **Visual Studio 2005**, and create a new Web site, using the language of your choice. ▪ Use the **ASP.NET Web Site** application template. ▪ Name the new Web site **NWindStockWeb**. ▪ Save the Web site in the default location. **Note** In Visual Studio 2005, to create a Web site, on the **File** menu, point to **New** and then click **Web site**. You do not use the **New Project** dialog as in Visual Studio .NET. Notice that, with ASP.NET 2.0, you can create a Web site in any folder on your PC. You do not need to host your application in an Internet Information Services (IIS) Web site while you develop it.
4. Create a connection to the Northwind database in Server Explorer.	▪ Open Server Explorer and click the **Connect to Database** button. ▪ If necessary, in the **Choose Data Source** dialog box, select **Microsoft SQL Server**, and then click **Continue**. ▪ Enter **london\sqlexpress** for the server name, and then select the **Northwind** database. ▪ Click **Test Connection**. If the connection succeeds, click **OK**. If not, seek assistance from the instructor.

(*continued*)

Tasks	Supporting information
5. Add a **SqlDataSource** and a data bound **GridView** to the **Default.aspx** page by dragging data fields from Server Explorer.	See the following resources in the Lab Toolkit: ■ *Working with the SqlDataSource Control* ■ *Northwind Traders Technical Specification: Stock Level Monitoring Application* ■ View the **Default.aspx** page in Design view. ■ Set its **Title** property as detailed in the technical specification. ■ Drag required fields from the **Suppliers** table in Server Explorer onto the form. This will create the required **SqlDataSource** and **GridView** controls. ■ Resize the **GridView** control to an appropriate width based on the user interface (UI) prototype graphic in the technical specification. **Note** Format settings for font color and grid styles will be added in a later exercise.
6. Test the application.	■ Run the project. **Note** ASP.NET 2.0 uses its own "light" Web server to debug applications. IIS is not required. ■ If prompted, modify Web.config to enable debugging. ■ When you have verified that the supplier data is displayed, close Internet Explorer to end the debugging session.

Exercise 2
Adding Interactivity to the Web Application

In this exercise, you will add functionality that will enable users to sort, page, and filter the stock data displayed in the Web application.

Scenario

After some usability testing, the beta testers for the stock management automation project have requested that you modify the stock level–monitoring application so that users can sort through the list of suppliers to make it easier to find one in particular. They would also like to be able to view a maximum of five suppliers at a time to avoid scrolling the page. Finally, because a Supplier Relationship Manager is assigned to each country, the project stakeholders would like to be able to filter the list of suppliers by country.

Tasks	Supporting information
1. Enable sorting.	■ Use the **GridView** control's smart tag to select the **Enable Sorting** check box. **Note** Smart tags are used in Visual Studio 2005 to enable quick access to common control configuration tasks. ■ Test the application and verify that you can sort the data by clicking a column heading.
2. Enable paging.	■ Open the **GridView** control's smart tag and select the **Enable Paging** check box. ■ View the properties of the **GridView** control, and note that you can control the number of records per page by setting the **PageSize** property. Set the **PageSize** property to **5**. ■ Expand the **PagerSettings** property, and note that the **Mode** property is used to control the navigation links for paging through data. Leave the **Mode** property with the default value of **Numeric**. ■ Test the application and verify that you can navigate through the data by clicking the page numbers at the bottom of the grid.

(continued)

Tasks	Supporting information
3. Implement filtering.	See the Lab Toolkit resource ■ *Northwind Traders Technical Specification: Stock Level Monitoring Application* ■ *Working with the SqlDataSource Control* ■ As shown in the UI prototype graphic in the technical specification, add to the form both a **Label** control displaying the text **Country** and a **TextBox** control. ■ Set the **(ID)** property of the **TextBox** control to **CountryTextBox**, and set its **AutoPostBack** property to **True**. Leave all other properties with their default values. ■ Click the **SqlDataSource** control's smart tag and then click **Configure Data Source**. ■ Add the following **Where** clause to the **Select** statement: `[Country] LIKE '%' + @Country + '%'` ■ To do this, configure the SelectedCountry parameter with the following properties: • **Column = Country** • **Operator = LIKE** • **Source = Control** • **ControlID = CountryTextBox** • **DefaultValue = %** ■ Test the query. When prompted for a parameter value, make sure Type is set to string, leave the parameter blank and click **OK** to verify that all rows are returned. ■ If you want, you can test the query again, this time providing a parameter such as USA. ■ On the **Test Query** page, click **Finish**. ■ Test the application and verify that you can filter the data by entering **USA** in the **Country** text box.

Exercise 3
Creating a Details View

In this exercise, you will add a **DetailsView** control, and configure the Web application so that users can select a supplier and view their supplied products.

Scenario

The management team is happy with the progress of the stock level–monitoring application so far. They would now like to be able to select a supplier and view the stock-level status for each of their supplied products.

Tasks	Supporting information
1. Enable selection of rows.	See the Lab Toolkit resource *How to Implement Master-Detail Data Binding with the GridView and DetailsView Controls.* ■ **Enable selection** for the **GridView** control. ■ Ensure that the SupplierID field provides the selected value for the **GridView** control. ■ Set the **SelectedIndex** property of the **GridView** control to **0** (to select the first row by default).
2. Add a **DetailsView** control to the page.	See the following resources in the Lab Toolkit: ■ *How to Implement Master-Detail Data Binding with the GridView and DetailsView Controls* ■ *Northwind Traders Technical Specification: Stock Level Monitoring Application* ■ Under the **GridView** control, press ENTER to create a blank line. ■ Drag a **DetailsView** control from the **Data** section of the **Toolbox** and drop it in the new blank line. ■ In the smart tag for the **DetailsView** control, select **New data source** from the **Choose Data Source** list. ■ Select **Database** and enter **ProductsData** in the **Specify an ID for the data source** box. Then click **OK**. ■ On the **Choose Your Data Connection** page, select **NorthwindConnectionString1** (this is the connection string generated when you created the first data source on the page), and then click **Next**. ■ On the **Configure the Select Statement** page, select the **Products** table, and then select the required columns as specified in the technical specification. ■ Add a **Where** clause to the query. The **Where** clause should filter the returned rows to those with a SupplierID that matches the **GridView1** control. A default value of **1** should be specified so that products for supplier 1 will be returned when no supplier is selected. ■ Test the query using the default parameter value. Once you have successfully tested the query, click **Finish**.

(continued)

Tasks	Supporting information
2. *(continued)*	■ Click the **DetailsView** control's smart tag and then select **Enable Paging**. ■ Set the **Width** property of the **DetailsView** control to match the UI prototype graphic in the technical specification. ■ Test the application, verify that you can select a supplier in the **GridView**, and then view its products in the **DetailsView**.
3. Format the controls.	See the Lab Toolkit resource *Northwind Traders Technical Specification: Stock Level Monitoring Application.* ■ Click the **GridView** control's smart tag and then select **Auto Format**. ■ Select the **Oceanica** style and then click **OK**. ■ Apply the same style to the **DetailsView** control. ■ In the **DetailsView** control's smart tag, click **Edit Templates**. ■ Select **Header Template**, and then click in the control's header template section and type **Products**. ■ On the **DetailsView** control's smart tag, click **End Template Editing**. ■ Test the application.

Exercise 4
Enabling Data Updates

In this exercise, you will refine the stock-monitoring application to enable updates to the data.

Scenario

The supplier relationship managers at Northwind Traders have asked you to implement functionality in the stock-monitoring application that will allow them to modify supplier and product details through the application.

Tasks	Supporting information
1. View the update statements for the Suppliers data source.	See the following resources in the Lab Toolkit: ■ *Working with the SqlDataSource Control* ■ *How to Implement Data Bound Updates* ■ *Northwind Traders Technical Specification: Stock Level Monitoring Application* ■ Click the smart tag for the **SqlDataSource1** control, and then click **Configure Data Source**. ■ Click **Next**, and then on the **Configure the Select Statement** page, select **Specify a custom SQL statement** or **stored procedure** and then click **Next**. ■ Click the **Update**, **Insert**, and **Delete** tabs to view the Transact-SQL statements generated when the **SqlDataSource** was created. ■ Click **Cancel** to close the wizard.
2. Enable editing in the **GridView** control.	■ Open the **GridView** control's smart tag and configure the control to allow users to modify existing records. ■ Ensure that only the fields specified in the technical specification are updateable.
3. Generate update statements for the products data.	■ Use the smart tag for the **ProductsData SqlDataSource** control to generate **Insert**, **Update** and **Delete** statements. To do this, on the **Configure the Select Statement** page, click the **Advanced** button. ■ In the **Advanced SQL Generation Options** dialog box, click **OK**. ■ Click **Next**, and in the **Test Query** page, click **Finish**.
4. Enable editing in the **DetailsView** control.	■ In the **DetailsView1** properties, set **AutoGenerateEditButton** to True, to allow users to modify existing records. ■ Ensure that only the fields specified in the technical specification are updateable.
5. Test the application.	■ Test the application by editing supplier 1, changing the **ContactName** to **Amy Anderson**. You can also change the UnitsInStock value of any product.

Exercise 5
Creating a Contacts List

In this exercise, you will add a **TreeView** control and bind it to an XML file.

Scenario

Supplier-Relationship Managers often need to call a contact at a supplier in order to query an outstanding order or to get information about product availability. The contact details for each supplier are currently stored in an .xml file. The Supplier-Relationship Managers would like to be able to view the supplier contacts in the stock level–monitoring application, and select a supplier to have their telephone numbers displayed.

Tasks	Supporting information
1. Add the contacts file to the Web site.	📄 See the Lab Toolkit resource *Data Binding with XML Data*. ▪ Use Windows Explorer to view the contents of the E:\Microsoft Learning\2364\Labfiles\Lab05a\Starter folder. ▪ Drag **Contacts.xml** and drop it in the App_Data folder in the Solution Explorer pane in Visual Studio. ▪ View the Contacts.xml file you have just added to the solution.
2. Create the contacts page.	▪ Right-click the project in Solution Explorer and click **Add New Item**. ▪ Select **Web Form** from the available templates and enter **Contacts.aspx** for the name. 📄 **Note** ASP.NET 2.0 offers a number of options when you add a new Web Form: ▪ You can select the language for the new Web Form. You can also mix Web Forms written in different programming languages in the same Web site in ASP.NET 2.0. ▪ You can choose to place server code in the same file as the persistence format code, or in a separate code-behind file. The default behavior is to put all code in a separate code-behind file. To change this behavior, you must de-select the **Place code in separate file** check box. ▪ You can create a Web Form that displays inside a master page by selecting the **Select Master Page** check box. This feature of ASP.NET 2.0 is the subject of Lab 5B. ▪ Click **Add**. ▪ Set the **Title** property of the new page to **Supplier Contacts**. ▪ Add a hyperlink control to **Default.aspx** (next to the **selectedCountry** TextBox) and set its **Text** property to **Contacts** and its **NavigateUrl** property to **Contacts.aspx**.
3. Add an **XmlDataSource** and **TreeView** to Default.aspx.	▪ View Contacts.aspx in Design view. ▪ Drag **Contacts.xml** from Solution Explorer and drop it on the page.

(*continued*)

Tasks	Supporting information
4. Configure the **TreeView** data bindings.	See the following resource in the Lab Toolkit: • *Data Binding with XML Data* • *Northwind Traders Technical Specification: Stock Level Monitoring Application* • Click the **TreeView** control's smart tag, and select **Edit TreeNode Databindings**. • Modify the data bindings such that the list is titled **Select a Contact**, and then set the **TreeView Contact** node **TextField** property to Name, and the **ValueField** to Phone.
5. Format the **TreeView** control.	• Click the **TreeView** control's smart tag, and select **Auto Format**. • In the list of formats, click **Contacts** and then click **OK**.

6. Add controls to display the phone number of the selected contact.	See the Lab Toolkit resource *Northwind Traders Technical Specification: Stock Level Monitoring Application*.
	
	• Drag two **Label** controls from the **Toolbox** onto the Contacts.aspx form, one to display **Phone:** for the text property, and the second to display the phone number of the selected contact, as described in the Technical Specification.
	
	• Set the second **Label** control's **(ID)** property to **phoneLabel** and its **Text** property to an empty string.
	
	• Double-click the **TreeView** control to create its **SelectedNodeChanged** event handler.
	
	Note Visual Studio 2005 includes code in the page file by default, but you can specify that a separate code-behind file should be used when you add a Web form to the project. Previous versions of Visual Studio .NET put code in a separate code-behind file by default.
	
	Visual Studio provides a **Server Code** view, which displays only your code. You can click the **Source** tab to see your code embedded in the HTML for the page.
	
	• Add the following code to the event handler:
	
	<pre>[Visual Basic .NET]
	phoneLabel.Text = TreeView1.SelectedNode.Value</pre><pre>[Visual C# .NET]
	phoneLabel.Text = TreeView1.SelectedNode.Value;</pre>

7. Test the application.	• Save all files. • Run the application. • Click the **Contacts** link. • Select a contact. Verify that the telephone number is displayed in the text box.

Lab 5B: Programming Master Pages, Site Navigation, and Themes

- Exercise 1: Creating Master and Content Pages
- Exercise 2: Creating Departmental Master Pages
- Exercise 3: Implementing Site Navigation
- Exercise 4: Implementing Themes and Skins

After completing this lab, you will be able to:

- Create Web applications, with consistent layouts that are modular and easy to maintain, using master pages.
- Create Web applications and make them highly navigable by using site navigation.
- Create Web applications and use themes to provide the applications with consistent, flexible, and easy-to-maintain appearances.

Important You can choose to program with either Visual C# or Visual Basic in this workshop. Code samples and lab solutions are provided in both programming languages. If you prefer, you can choose to perform some labs using one programming language, and perform others using the other language. However, once you start a lab, you should complete all the exercises in that lab using the same programming language.

Lab Setup

1. If LONDON Virtual PC is still running after the previous lab, on the **Action** menu, click **Close**. The **Action** menu is visible when the Virtual PC is running in windowed mode, but not when it is running full-screen. If you are running the Virtual PC full-screen, press <RIGHT>ALT+ENTER to switch to windowed mode.

   In the Close window, select **Turn off and delete changes** and then click **OK**.

2. Start LONDON Virtual PC.

Lab Toolkit Resources

Use the following Lab Toolkit resources to help you complete this lab:

■ Northwind Traders Technical Specification: Intranet Portal Integration

■ Creating Web Applications Using Master Pages

■ Creating Modular Web Application Layouts Using Nested Master Pages

■ Creating Navigable Web Applications Using Visual Studio 2005

■ Controlling the Appearance of Web Applications Using Themes

■ Creating Custom Page Themes

Estimated time to complete this lab: **90 minutes**

Lab Solution Files

There are Visual Basic and Visual C# solution files associated with the labs in this workshop. The lab solution files are located in the folder E:\Microsoft Learning\2364\Labfiles\Lab05b\Solution on the Virtual PCs.

Exercise 1
Creating Master and Content Pages

In this exercise, you will use master and content pages to create the basic structure of the Northwind Portal mockup according to the specification supplied by Nicole Holliday, senior developer at Northwind Traders.

Scenario

You are a developer working for Northwind Traders. The intranet portal project is in trouble and will not be delivered on time, meaning that the Automated Supplier Reordering Application cannot be tested in the new portal environment. You have been asked to create a mockup of the portal that encapsulates many of its most important features. This will allow your team to continue to make progress with its development and testing while waiting for the real portal to be delivered.

The first step is to implement the basic structure of the Northwind Portal using a master page and create a default home page.

Tasks	Supporting information
1. Log on to LONDON using the Student account.	▪ The current password for the Student account is **Pa$$w0rd**.
2. Open the Lab Toolkit and read the Program Technical Specification.	See the following resource on the **Scenario** tab in the Lab Toolkit: *Northwind Traders Technical Specification: Intranet Portal Integration*.
3. Start Visual Studio 2005 and create a new Web site using the language of your choice. Name the project **NorthwindPortal**.	▪ Create a Web site using the following settings: • Template: **Empty Web Site** • Location: **C:\Websites\NorthwindPortal** • Language: Your choice
4. Create the Northwind Portal master page.	See the Lab Toolkit resource *Creating Web Applications Using Master Pages*. ▪ Add a new page to the project using the following settings: • Template: **Master Page** • Name: **Northwind.master** • Language: Your choice
5. Review and edit the Northwind.master page.	▪ Verify that the **Northwind.master** page is opened in Source view and review the standard content: • Notice the **@Master** directive. • Notice that the overall structure of the master page is the same as a standard .aspx file and includes the standard set of tags: <html>, <head>, <body>, and <form>. • Notice the structure of the **asp:contentplaceholder** declaration contained within the <form> element. ▪ Switch to the Design view and delete **ContentPlaceHolder1**. You will create others once you have the page structure in place.

(continued)

Tasks	Supporting information
6. Specify the layout of the Northwind Portal master page.	See the following resource on the **Scenario** tab in the Lab Toolkit: *Northwind Traders Technical Specification: Intranet Portal Integration.*
	▪ To specify the layout of the Northwind Portal master page switch back to Source view.
	▪ Create a table on the Northwind.master page by using the structure specified in the Technical Specification. This table establishes the standard layout for all portal pages.
	▪ Create the table by copying the predefined table definition from the file E:\Microsoft Learning\2364\Labfiles\Lab05b\Starter\ NorthwindPortalMasterTable.htm to the <form> element in the Northwind.master page. The table definition contains CSS class attributes that you will use later in this lab.
	▪ Notice that each cell in the table contains text that identifies its purpose (or region name) as described in the Technical Specification.
7. Create the standard content that will appear on all portal pages.	▪ To create the standard content that will appear on all portal pages right-click the project in Solution Explorer and then point to **Add Folder**. Click **Regular Folder**, and name it **Images**.
	▪ Right-click the **Images** folder and then click **Add Existing Item**. Add the file E:\Microsoft Learning\2364\Labfiles\Lab05b\Starter\ NorthwindHeader.jpg to the project.
	▪ Open the Northwind.master page in Design view.
	▪ Drag an **Image** control to the Header region of the page.
	● Delete the text in the **Header** region.
	● Configure the **Image** control to display the NorthwindHeader.jpg file.
	▪ Drag a **ContentPlaceHolder** control to the Application region of the page.
	● Delete the text in the **Application** region.
	● Rename the **(ID)** of **ContentPlaceHolder** control to **Application**.
	▪ Drag a **ContentPlaceHolder** control to the Department region of the page.
	● Delete the text in the **Department** region.
	● Rename the **(ID)** of **ContentPlaceHolder** control to **Department**.
	▪ Leave all other table cells containing only the text of their region name for now.
8. Create default content for the portal's Department region.	▪ To create default content for the portal's **Department** region drag a Label control onto the **ContentPlaceHolder** control in the portal's **Department** region. The content of this label will be displayed by all pages that do not provide alternate content.
	▪ Set the **Text** property of the **Label** control to **Welcome to the Northwind Intranet Portal Mockup** and increase the **Font.Size** property to **X-Large**.

(*continued*)

Tasks	Supporting information
9. Create the default Northwind Portal home page.	See the Lab Toolkit resource *Creating Web Applications Using Master Pages*. ■ To create the default Northwind Portal home page right-click on the **Northwind.master** page and then click **Add Content Page**. The Default.aspx file created is a content page for the **Northwind.master** page and will be the default homepage for the portal. ■ Review the content of **Default.aspx** in the **Source** view. Notice that: • The page currently contains the @Page directives as well as two empty content placeholders.to represent the content placeholders specified on the **Northwind.master** page. • The **masterPageFile** attribute in the @ **Page** directive refers to the **Northwind.master** page.
10. Add content to the Northwind Portal home page.	See the Lab Toolkit resource *Creating Web Applications Using Master Pages*. ■ To add content to the Northwind Portal home page copy the file **E:\Microsoft Learning\2364\Labfiles\Lab05b\Starter\ NorthwindCompass.jpg** to the **Images** folder, and add it to the project. ■ Open the **Default.aspx** page in Design view. ■ Notice that the content of the **Northwind.master** page is displayed, but only the regions containing **ContentPlaceHolders** are editable. ■ Drag an **Image** control from the **Toolbox** and drop it onto the **ContentPlaceHolder** control "Content-Content1(Custom)" that represents the portal's Application region. ■ Configure the **Image** control to display the **NorthwindCompass.jpg** file. ■ Click **Default to Master's Content** on the shortcut menu for the **ContentPlaceHolder** control "Content-Content2(Custom)" that represents the portal's Department region. This causes the control to display the contents of the **ContentPlaceHolder** on the master page. ■ Switch to Source view and review the structure of the content page. Notice that: • The content page now contains a **Content** control with its **ContentPlaceHolderID** attribute set to the value "Application." This is the **ID** of the **ContentPlaceHolder** control declared in the **Northwind.master** page that represents the portal's Application region. • The **Content** control is a top-level element in the page.

(continued)

Tasks	Supporting information
11. Configure the **Northwind.master** page as the Web application's default master page.	See the Lab Toolkit resource *Creating Web Applications Using Master Pages*. ■ Add a new Web Configuration File (Web.config) to the root folder of the project. ■ Open the Web.config file. ■ Add the following tag as a child of the to the <system.web> tag: `<pages masterPageFile="Northwind.master" />` Although the **Default.aspx** page explicitly specifies **Northwind.master** as its master page, it is good practice to specify a default master page where one exists in case other developers fail to specify a master page for their content pages. **Important** The **masterPageFile** attribute in the **pages** tag of the Web.config file is case-sensitive.
12. Build the project.	■ Build the NorthwindPortal project, resolving any build errors that occur.
13. Test the application.	■ Notice how the **Default.aspx** page displayed in the client browser represents a merged view of the content declared in the **NorthwindPortal.master** and **Default.aspx**.

Exercise 2
Creating Departmental Master Pages

In this exercise, you will use nested master pages to modularize the layout of the Northwind Portal mockup.

Scenario

A goal of the Northwind Portal is to ensure consistency and simplify ongoing maintenance without constraining the capabilities of departments to implement the applications they need. As such, the portal allocates two regions for departmental use. The first region is for general departmental content, and the other is for application-specific content. The Portal Development Team plans to advise departments that have multiple applications to use nested master pages to provide the general department content and application-specific content pages to provide application content.

Knowing that the purchasing department will have multiple applications, you need to implement a nested master page in which to test the Automated Supplier Reordering Application. You also know that Visual Studio 2005 does not support the graphic editing of nested master and content pages, so you will develop the nested master page by itself before binding it to its master.

Tasks	Supporting information
1. Create a master page for the Purchasing department.	See the Lab Toolkit resource *Creating Web Applications Using Master Pages*. ▪ Add a new page to the project using the following settings: • Template: **Master Page** • Name: **Purchasing.master** • Language: Your choice
2. Configure the content place-holder on the Purchasing master page to represent the portal's Application region.	▪ Open the **Purchasing.master** page in Design view. ▪ Change the **(ID)** property of the existing **ContentPlaceHolder** control from "ContentPlaceHolder1" to "Application."
3. Create default content for the Application region of the Purchasing master page.	▪ Copy the file E:\Microsoft Learning\2364\Labfiles\Lab05b\Starter\ **Purchasing.jpg** to the **Images** folder, and then add it to the project. ▪ Drag an **Image** control from the **Toolbox** and drop it onto the **ContentPlaceHolder** control that represents the portal's Application region. ▪ Configure the **Image** control to display the Purchasing.jpg file.
4. Create a content page to represent an example purchasing department application.	▪ Add another new page to the project using the following settings: • Template: **Web Form** • Name: **SupplierApp.aspx** • Language: Your choice and then enable **Select master page** • Master page: **Purchasing.master**

(continued)

Tasks	Supporting information

5. Create and configure a data source to provide access to the **Suppliers** table in the Northwind database.	▪ Open **SupplierApp.aspx** in Design view.
	
	▪ From the **Toolbox**, drag a **SqlDataSource** component onto the **Content** control "Content-Content 1(Custom)" that represents the portal's Application region.
	
	▪ Configure the **SqlDataSource** component project using the following settings:
	  • Data Source: **Microsoft SQL Server**
	  • Server: **London\sqlexpress**
	  • Database: **Northwind**
	  • Configure Select Statement: Select all columns from the **Suppliers** table.

6. Create and configure a **GridView** to display details from the **Suppliers** table.	▪ Drag a **GridView** control from the **Toolbox** and drop it alongside the **SqlDataSource** component. ▪ Configure the **GridView** to connect to the **SqlDataSource** you just created. ▪ Enable paging and sorting on the **GridView** control.
7. Build and test the **SupplierApp.aspx** page.	See the Lab Toolkit resource *Creating Modular Web Application Layouts Using Nested Master Pages*. ▪ Before making the **Purchasing.master** page into a nested master page and losing the ability to edit it and **SupplierApp.aspx** graphically, it makes sense to ensure that the pages work correctly. ▪ Notice that the **SupplierApp.aspx** shown in the client browser contains only a table with information from the Suppliers table. The Purchasing.jpg image has been replaced by the **GridView** specified by the **SupplierApp.aspx** content page. **Tip** If you select an .aspx file in Solution Explorer and press F5 or CTRL+F5, Visual Studio 2005 will run the selected page and not Default.aspx.

(continued)

Tasks	Supporting information

8. Convert the **Purchasing.master** page into a nested master page.	See the following resources in the Lab Toolkit:
	
	 ▪ *Creating Modular Web Application Layouts Using Nested Master Pages*
	
	 ▪ *Creating Web Applications Using Master Pages*
	
	▪ Open the **Purchasing.master** page in Source view.
	
	▪ Configure **Purchasing.master** to use **Northwind.master** as its master page by adding a **MasterPageFile** attribute to the **@Master** directive in **Purchasing.master**.
	
	▪ Delete everything from **Purchasing.master** except the **@Master** directive and the **asp:contentplaceholder** declaration. This includes deleting the **<html>**, **<head>**, **<body>**, and **<form>** elements that currently encapsulate the **asp:contentplaceholder** declaration.
	
	▪ Type in a new **Content** control declaration that encapsulates the existing **ContentPlaceHolder** control. Configure the **Content** control as follows:
	
	`<asp:Content ContentPlaceHolderID="Application"`
	`   ID="Content1" Runat="Server">`
	`   <!-- Existing asp:contentplaceholder element here -->`
	`</asp:Content>`

9. Provide default department-specific content for the portal's Department region.	See the Lab Toolkit resource *Creating Modular Web Application Layouts Using Nested Master Pages*.
	
	▪ Type in the declaration for a second **Content** control into the **Purchasing.master** page below the one you added in the previous step. This will provide content for the portal's Department region. Configure the **Content** control as follows:
	
	`<asp:Content ContentPlaceHolderID="Department"`
	`   ID="Content2" Runat="Server">`
	`   Welcome to the Purchasing Department.`
	`</asp:Content>`

10. Build the project.	▪ Build the NorthwindPortal project, resolving any build errors that occur.
11. Test the application.	▪ Execute the **SupplierApp.aspx** page. ▪ Notice that you now have nested master pages the **SupplierApp.aspx** page displayed in the client browser represent a merged view of the content declared in the **Northwind.master**, **Purchasing.master**, and **SupplierApp.aspx** pages. ▪ Notice how the default content specified in **Northwind.master** for the portal's Department region has been replaced by the content specified in the **Purchasing.master** page.

Exercise 3
Implementing Site Navigation

In this exercise, you will add navigation support to the Northwind Portal mockup using ASP.NET site navigation.

Scenario

The Northwind Portal design identifies two regions dedicated to site navigation. The Menu region will contain an expandable treelike menu that provides the user with a visual representation of the portal's logical structure and allows the user to jump to department home pages and key application pages. The Breadcrumb region will contain a breadcrumb control that shows the users where they are in the Web site's logical hierarchy and allows them to jump to higher levels with a single click.

Tasks	Supporting information

1. Create a sample home page for the Purchasing department.	See the Lab Toolkit resource *Creating Web Applications Using Master Pages*.
	
	■ Add a new content page to the project using the following settings:
	  • Template: **Web Form**
	  • Name: **Purch.aspx**
	  • Language: Your choice
	  • Master page: **Purchasing.master**

2. Create placeholder pages for the Sales department.	See the Lab Toolkit resource *Creating Web Applications Using Master Pages*.
	
	■ Add another new content page to the project using the following settings:
	  • Template: **Web Form**
	  • Name: **Sales.aspx**
	  • Language: Your choice
	  • Master page: **Northwind.master**

3. Add an XML site map file to the project.	See the Lab Toolkit resource *Creating Navigable Web Applications Using Visual Studio 2005*. ■ Copy the file **E:\Microsoft Learning\2364\Labfiles\Lab05b\ Starter\web.sitemap** to the root folder of the project and add it to the project. ■ Open the **web.sitemap** file and review its content. ■ Using the structure of the Sales siteMapNode and its child nodes as a guide, create a child node for the Purchasing siteMapNode that provides a connection to the SupplierApp.aspx file.

(continued)

Tasks	Supporting information
4. Add a new navigation data source to the Northwind Portal master page.	See the Lab Toolkit resource *Creating Navigable Web Applications Using Visual Studio 2005.* ■ Open the **Northwind.master** file in Design view. ■ Drag a **SiteMapDataSource** component from the **Toolbox**, under Data, and drop it into the portal's Menu region. Delete the text placeholder from the Menu region. ■ The **SiteMapDataSource** component automatically uses the default site navigation provider, which obtains site map data from the web.sitemap file in the application root.
5. Enable menu-based navigation support in the Northwind Portal.	See the Lab Toolkit resource *Creating Navigable Web Applications Using Visual Studio 2005.* ■ Drag a **TreeView** control from the **Toolbox**, under Navigation, and drop it in the portal's Menu region. ■ Configure the **TreeView** to connect to the **SiteMapDataSource** you just created. ■ Notice that the content of the web.sitemap file is automatically displayed in Design view once the **TreeView** is bound to the **SiteMapDataSource**.
6. Enable breadcrumb-based navigation support in the Northwind Portal.	See the Lab Toolkit resource *Creating Navigable Web Applications Using Visual Studio 2005.* ■ Drag a **SiteMapPath** control from the **Toolbox**, under Navigation, and drop it in the portal's Breadcrumb region. Remove the text from the region. ■ The **SiteMapPath** control automatically uses the default site navigation provider, which obtains site map data from the web.sitemap file in the application root.
7. Build the project.	■ Build the NorthwindPortal project, resolving any build errors that occur.
8. Test the application.	■ Experiment with the navigation capabilities provided by the **SiteMapPath** and **TreeView** controls by jumping between the Northwind Home, Purchasing, and Supplier menu items. ■ Notice how by placing the navigation controls in the **Northwind.master** page you have enabled navigation support on all content pages. This means that navigation for your entire site is maintained centrally. ■ Notice how the breadcrumb control automatically determines where in the logical site hierarchy the user is.

Exercise 4 (Optional)
Implementing Themes and Skins

If you have time, work through this exercise in which you will use themes to set a standard look and feel for the Northwind Portal mockup.

Scenario

Having successfully implemented the layout and navigation capabilities of the Northwind Portal in your mockup, you now turn your attention to addressing the portal's visual appearance, which is currently unsatisfactory.

On initial implementation, the Northwind Portal will use themes to support two different appearances that will be available to users. The themes are named North and South. The mechanism for controlling the user's theme configuration is yet to be determined by the Portal Development Team, but the themes themselves are relatively well developed.

The next step is to implement the themes with the Portal mockup and ensure that they create a consistent appearance across the portal. You must also create the skins required by the Legal department, which have not yet been included in the North and South themes provided to you.

Tasks	Supporting information

1. Install the North and South themes.	See the Lab Toolkit resource *Controlling the Appearance of Web Applications using Themes.*
	
	■ There is an App_Themes folder in the root folder of the NorthwindPortal project. This is where ASP.NET 2.0 will look for all page themes.
	
	■ Under the App_Themes folder, add a North theme folder and a South theme folder.
	
	■ Copy the contents of the North and South folders from E:\Microsoft Learning\2364\Labfiles\Lab05b\Starter to each of the North and South themes folders. You do not need to do anything else to add themes to a project. ASP.NET will automatically identify available themes at run time based on the immediate subfolders of the Themes folder.
	
	■ Review the contents of the North and South themes. Notice that:
	
	  • Each theme contains the same set of skin files, but each skin file contains different property settings for the controls they affect.
	
	  • Each theme contains a CSS style sheet and images tailored to suit the theme.

(*continued*)

Tasks	Supporting information
2. Use named skins on **Image** controls.	See the Lab Toolkit resource *Controlling the Appearance of Web Applications using Themes*.
	■ Each **Image** control needs to display a different image that is tailored to the active theme. The theme-specific images are contained in an Images subfolder of the theme folders.
	■ Open the Image.skin file from within the North or South themes and review its content. Notice that:
	• There are three named skins. This is because each **Image** control in the portal needs to display a different image.
	• The **ImageURL** property for each skin specifies a path relative to the theme folder, not relative to the application root.
	■ Using Design view (or Source view for the nested master page), notice that the **SkinID** properties of all **Image** controls in the portal is as follows:
	• The **Image** control in the Header region of the **Northwind.master** page uses the skin named **NorthwindHeader**.
	• The **Image** control in the Application region of the **Default.aspx** page uses the skin named **NorthwindCompass**.
	• The **Image** control in the Application region of the **Purchasing.master** page uses the skin named **Purchasing**.
3. Populate the portal's Account region with sample content.	■ Open **Northwind.master** in Design view.
	■ Drag a **LoginName** control from the **Toolbox** and drop it in the portal's Account region, making sure to delete the text from the region.
4. Add a skin for the **LoginName** control.	See the Lab Toolkit resource *Creating Custom Page Themes*.
	■ When you look in the North or South themes, you will notice that there is no skin file for **LoginName** controls (that is, there is no file named LoginName.skin).
	■ Create a new skin file in the North theme folder and name it **LoginName.skin**.
	■ Open the **LoginName.skin** file and add a default skin that will set the properties of **LoginName** controls as follows:
	• Runat: "**Server**"
	• FormatString: "**Active user: {0}**"
	• BackColor: "**#8080FF**"
	• ForeColor: "**#E0E0E0**"

(*continued*)

Tasks	Supporting information
4. (*continued*)	▪ Repeat the same process for the South theme but switch the values of the BackColor and ForeColor. **Tip** It is easier to create a skin if you first add the desired control to a page in Design view and configure it the way you want it to appear. Then switch to Source view, copy the control's declaration, paste it to the skin file, and then remove the properties that should not be present.
5. Populate the portal's News/Info region with sample content.	▪ Open **Northwind.master** in Design view. ▪ Drag a **ListBox** control from the Toolbox and drop it in the portal's News/Info region, making sure to delete the text from the region. ▪ Add some static items to the **Items** collection of the **ListBox** to represent news items for the purpose of testing.

6. Populate the portal's Legal region with sample content.	See the Lab Toolkit resource *Controlling the Appearance of Web Applications using Themes*.
	
	▪ Drag a **Button** control from the Toolbox and drop it on the portal's Legal region, making sure to delete the text from the region.
	▪ Set the following properties of the **Button** control:
	  • Text: **Legal**
	  • SkinID: **LegalLink**

7. Create the LegalLink skin for a **Button**.	See the Lab Toolkit resource *Creating Custom Page Themes*.
	
	▪ Open the Button.skin file in the North theme.
	▪ Notice that there is a default skin for a **Button** control, but the Legal department requires the button providing the link to their information to stand out from the rest of the portal.
	▪ Create a new skin with the following settings:
	  • SkinID: **LegalLink**
	  • Runat: **Server**
	  • BackColor: **#FFFF80**
	  • ForeColor: **#FF0000**
	▪ Copy the **LegalLink** skin definition to the **Button.skin** file in the South theme. This will ensure that the Legal button has a consistent appearance across both the North and South themes.

(continued)

Tasks	Supporting information
8. Configure North as the default theme.	See the Lab Toolkit resource *Controlling the Appearance of Web Applications using Themes*. ■ Open the **Web.config** file. ■ Set North as the default theme by adding a **theme** attribute to the **pages** element. **Important** The **theme** attribute in the **pages** node of the Web.config file is case-sensitive.
9. Build the project.	■ Build the NorthwindPortal project, resolving any build errors that occur.
10. Test the application.	■ Navigate through the pages that exist in the portal mockup and notice: • The effect the theme has had on the different controls, especially the **GridView** on the **SuppliersApp.aspx** page. • CSS classes used in the original table definition are picked up from the style sheet in the theme. • The text of the **SiteMapPath** control is different from the rest of the portal because no skin exists for this type of control. • The static items you placed in the **ListBox** control in the portal's News/Info region have been replaced by items accidentally left in the **ListBox** skin definition. ■ The Portal development team has yet to decide how they want to allow people to change themes, but the effect can be simulated manually. To do so, change the default theme to South and notice how the appearance of the entire portal is changed with almost no effort. You can make this change to Web.config while the application is being used; then, refresh your browser. ■ Look again at the **SuppliersApp.aspx** page and notice that there is no supplier information in the table. This is because the **GridView** skin in the South theme is configured incorrectly with the **ForeColor** property of the **RowStyle** being the same as the **BackColor**. You can fix this by changing the **ForeColor** property of the **RowStyle** to **#E0E0E0**. You can fix this while the application is still active and the change will take effect when the page is next refreshed. **Additional Information** When giving users the ability to configure the theme of their portal, you must address two issues: remembering the user's preference and implementing it. Remembering the user's preference involves storing the name of the theme the user wants to use. This name can be stored directly in a database or folder, or by using the new personalization capabilities of ASP.NET 2.0. Implementing the user's preference requires you to set the **Page.Theme** property to the desired theme name in the **Page_PreInit** method of every page.

Lab 5C: Membership and Role Management in ASP.NET 2.0

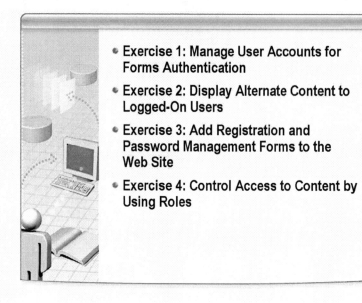

- Exercise 1: Manage User Accounts for Forms Authentication
- Exercise 2: Display Alternate Content to Logged-On Users
- Exercise 3: Add Registration and Password Management Forms to the Web Site
- Exercise 4: Control Access to Content by Using Roles

After completing this lab, you will be able to:

- Manage users by using the login controls.
- Manage user credentials and role groups.
- Manage a Web site by using the ASP.NET Web Site Administration tool.

Important You can choose to program with either Microsoft Visual C# or Visual Basic in this workshop. Code samples and lab solutions are provided in both programming languages. If you prefer, you can choose to perform some labs using one programming language, and perform others using the other language. However, once you start a lab, you should complete all the exercises in that lab using the same programming language.

Lab setup

For this lab, you will use the LONDON Virtual PC.

To prepare for this lab:

1. If LONDON Virtual PC is still running after the previous lab, on the **Action** menu, click **Close**. The **Action** menu is visible when the Virtual PC is running in windowed mode, but not when it is running full-screen. If you are running the Virtual PC full-screen, press <RIGHT>ALT+ENTER to switch to windowed mode.

2. In the Close window, select **Turn off and delete changes** and then click **OK**.

3. Start up the LONDON Virtual PC.

4. Then the LONDON Virtual PC has started up, log on as **Student** with a password of **Pa$$w0rd**.

5. Click the **Labfiles** Toolbar at the bottom right of the screen and navigate to **Lab05c\Setup**.

6. Click **Install.cmd** to setup the Virtual PC for this lab. This command file installs the starter code in Microsoft Visual SourceSafe® in preparation for the lab.

7. Enter the Administrator's password when prompted, which is **Pa$$w0rd**.

8. Press any key to exit the setup command procedure.

Lab Toolkit resources

Use the following Lab Toolkit resources to help you complete this lab:

- Northwind Traders Technical Specification: Stock Web Site
- Managing Security with the ASP.NET Web Site Administration Tool
- Programming the Login Controls

Estimated time to complete this lab: **75 minutes**

Lab solution files

There are Visual Basic and Visual C# solution files associated with the labs in this workshop. The lab solution files are located on the LONDON Virtual PC in the folder E:\Microsoft Learning\2364\ Labfiles\Lab05c\Solution.

Exercise 1
Manage User Accounts for Forms Authentication

In this exercise, you will force users to log on to view part of the Web site's content. You will manage user account credentials using the ASP.NET Web Site Administration tool.

Scenario

Your team is working on a Web site for Northwind Traders. A prototype of the Web site has already been completed, but at present there are no login controls that limit access to restricted content, so all users can view any page of the Web site. You will implement proper authorization controls on the site so that only logged-on users can view certain pages.

The first step is to restrict access to some of the site content to logged-on users, and to manage user accounts using the ASP.NET Web Site Administration tool.

Tasks	Supporting information
1. Open the Lab Toolkit and read the Program Technical Specification.	See the Lab Toolkit resource *Northwind Traders Technical Specification: Stock Web Site*.
2. Start Microsoft Visual Studio 2005 and open the partially completed Web site from Microsoft Visual SourceSafe®.	■ To start Microsoft Visual Studio, in London Virtual machine, click Start, and then click **Microsoft Visual Studio 2005 Beta 2**. ■ On the **Tools** menu select **Options**. ■ In the **Options** dialog box, expand **Projects and Solutions** and select **General**. ■ In the **Visual Studio project locations** textbox enter **C:\Websites** and click **OK**. ■ On the **File** menu, point to **Open**, and then click **Project/Solution**. ■ In the **Open Project** dialog box, click **My SourceSafe (LAN)**, and then click **SourceSafeDB**. ■ In the **Log Onto Visual SourceSafe Database** dialog box, enter the user name **Student**, leave the password field empty, leave the Database as **SourceSafeDB**, and then click **OK**. ■ In the **Open Project** dialog box, browse to **Lab05c\{language}\StockMaintenenance** , where {language} is **CS** or **VB** according to your preference, and double-click on **StockMaintenance.sln**. ■ In the **Source Control** dialog box, click **OK**. The rest of the files in the solution will be retrieved from the source control asynchronously.

(continued)

Tasks	Supporting information
3. Familiarize yourself with the application.	■ In Solution Explorer, expand the **project node** and then click **default.aspx**. ■ On the **Debug** menu, click **Start Debugging**. ■ Try out the different pages of the application. Notice how all pages are available to all users.

4. Use the ASP.NET Web Site Administration Tool to configure Forms authentication for the Web site.	See the Lab Toolkit resource *Managing Security with the ASP.NET Web Site Administration Tool*.
	
	■ In this task, you use the **ASP.NET Web Site Administration Tool** to edit this application's Web.config file. You must check this file out from Visual SourceSafe before running the ASP.NET Web Site Administration Tool. To check out a file, use one of two techniques:
	
	   ● Open the file and make a change to it. Visual Studio checks out the file from Visual SourceSafe automatically.
	
	   ● Alternatively, right-click the file in Solution Explorer and then click **Check Out for Edit**. You can enter a comment in the **Check Out For Edit** box and then click **Check Out**.
	
	■ In the **ASP.NET Web Site Administration Tool**, on the **Security** page, click the **Select Authentication Type** link to use the Security Setup Wizard to configure access control for users accessing the Web site from the Internet.
	
	■ After you have configured Forms authentication for this application, open the **Web.config** file.
	
	Notice the line that says <authentication mode="Forms" />. The ASP.NET Web Site Administration Tool added this line. You could have edited the Web.config file directly, but the ASP.NET Web Site Administration Tool allows you to make configuration changes without knowing the specific syntax required in the Web.config file.

(*continued*)

Tasks	Supporting information
5. Create the Login form.	See the following resources in the Lab Toolkit: <ul><li>*Northwind Traders Technical Specification: Stock Web Site*</li><li>*Programming the Login Controls*</li></ul> ▪ Add a new Web Form called **login.aspx** to the project. Make sure you check **Select master page** in the **Add New Item** box; select **sitetemplate.master** as the master page. ▪ Switch to Design view, and then drag a **Login** control onto the Content area. ▪ Open the **Common Login Tasks** smart tag and click **Auto Format** to format the control using the **Elegant** style, and then resize the control to fill the Content area.
6. Deny access to anonymous users to content in the ProductReorders folder.	See the Lab Toolkit resource *Managing Security with the ASP.NET Web Site Administration Tool*. ▪ Use the ASP.NET Web Site Administration Tool to deny access to anonymous users to ProductReorders folder.
7. Test the application.	▪ Notice how you are redirected to login.aspx if you request the Reorder Products page.
8. Use the ASP.NET Web Site Administration Tool to add users.	See the Lab Toolkit resource *Managing Security with the ASP.NET Web Site Administration Tool*. ▪ In the ASP.NET Web Site Administration Tool, create some user accounts to test with. **Note** While creating users, do note that the only password accepted is either 'P@ssw0rd' or 'Pa$$w0rd'.
9. Test the application.	▪ Request either the Reorder Products or the Site Reports pages and enter the credentials of a user account you just created. You can now view these pages.

Exercise 2
Display Alternate Content to Logged-On Users

In this exercise, you will add a link to the home page that allows users to log on. You will display a message at the top of every page that shows whether the current user is logged on or logged off. You will write code that determines whether the current user is logged on or is anonymous, and you will limit the display of product details data that is shown to anonymous users.

Scenario

Northwind Traders wants to encourage members of the public to register on the Web site. One step towards this goal is to allow logged-on users to view details about the suppliers of products stocked by Northwind, whereas anonymous users will not be able to view this information.

A message must be displayed at the top of every page on the Web site to show whether the current user is logged on or off.

Tasks	Supporting information
1. Create a Login/Logout link on the page header.	See the Lab Toolkit resource *Programming the Login Controls*. ▪ Use a **LoginStatus** control. Place it in the right-hand cell on the header area of the sitetemplate.master page. ▪ Set the **align** property of the table cell where you just placed the **LoginStatus** control to **center**. ▪ In the Source view of the page, add a tag before the **LoginStatus** control definition to insert a blank line before it. ▪ Set the **LoginImageUrl** and **LogoutImageUrl** properties to **login.gif** and **logout.gif** respectively. These images are in the Images subfolder.
2. Display a suitable message to logged-in/logged-out users.	See the following resources in the Lab Toolkit: ▪ *Northwind Traders Technical Specification: Stock Web Site* ▪ *Programming the Login Controls* ▪ Place a **LoginView** control underneath the **LoginStatus** control. ▪ Edit the **LoggedInTemplate** view. ▪ Drag an HTML **<DIV>** control onto the **LoggedInTemplate** view. Set the **(id)** property to **Whitetext**, which is a suitable style in the CSS stylesheet that is embedded in this Master page (see the Source view to view the CSS stylesheet). ▪ Inside the **<DIV>**, create a message for logged-on users that says **Welcome, {username}!**. Use the **LoginName** control to display the current username. ▪ Edit the **Anonymoustemplate** view. ▪ Drag a **<DIV>** control onto the **Anonymoustemplate** view and set its **(id)** property to **Whitetext**. ▪ Set the message for anonymous users to be **You are not logged on**.

(continued)

Tasks	Supporting information
3. Test the application.	▪ You should be able to log on and off by using the link on the page header. The message underneath changes according to your current status. ▪ Notice that the new controls are in the Master page, so they appear on all pages in the Web site.
4. Display limited product details to anonymous users.	▪ Create a **Page_Load** event handler for **Products.aspx**. ▪ Code an **if** statement that tests to determine if the user is **logged on**. An easy test for this is to see if the **User.Identity.Name** property is set to a string value (the user is logged on), or to a null string (user is anonymous). ▪ If the user is **anonymous**, set the **Visible** property to **False** for columns 1, 3, 6, and 7 of **GridView1**.
5. Test the application.	▪ Anonymous users see only limited product details. ▪ **Logged-on** users see full product details.

Exercise 3
Add Registration and Password Management Forms to the Web Site

In this exercise, you will add Web forms to the site to allow users to register, to reset their own passwords, and to retrieve a forgotten password.

Scenario

At present, you must register all users with the ASP.NET Web Site Administration Tool. This is clearly not practical for large numbers of users. You must add pages to the site to allow anonymous users to register on the site and to be e-mailed a lost password, and you must add another page to allow logged-on users to change their password.

Tasks	Supporting information
1. Create a registration page.	See the following resources in the Lab Toolkit: ■ *Northwind Traders Technical Specification: Stock Web Site* ■ *Programming the Login Controls* ■ Add a new Web Form to the project and name it **register.aspx**. In the **Add New Item** box, make sure **Select master page** is selected and then select **sitetemplate.master** as the master page. ■ Switch to **Design** view, and then drag a **CreateUserWizard** control onto the Content area. ■ Set the **ContinueDestinationPageUrl** property to **Default.aspx**. ■ On the **Common CreateUserWizard Tasks** smart tag, click **AutoFormat** to format the control using the **Elegant** style, and then resize the control to fill the Content area.

2. Add a link to the header to allow anonymous users to register.	See the following resources in the Lab Toolkit:
	■ *Northwind Traders Technical Specification: Stock Web Site*
	■ *Programming the Login Controls*
	
	■ Open **siteTemplate.Master** for editing.
	
	■ Cut the **LoginStatus** control that you added into the header during the last exercise. Open the **LoggedInTemplate** of the **LoginView** control you added in Exercise 2 and paste the **LoginStatus** control into it, in front of the message text you added previously. Add a
	 to move the message onto the line below the **LoginStatus** control.
	
	■ Paste the **LoginStatus** control into the **AnonymousTemplate** in a similar fashion.
	
	■ Edit the AnonymousTemplate:
	  • Drag a **Hyperlink** control from the **Toolbox** and place it to the right of the **LoginStatus** control.
	  • Set the **ImageUrl** property of the **Hyperlink** to ~/Images/Register.gif.
	  • Set the **NavigateUrl** property of the **Hyperlink** to Register.aspx.

(continued)

Tasks	Supporting information
3. Test the application.	▪ Check that when you are not logged on, you can click the **Register** button on the toolbar, and register yourself as a user.
	▪ Notice that the application automatically logs you on after you have completed the New User registration.
	▪ Check that the **Register** button is not visible when the user is logged on.
4. Allow users to retrieve lost passwords.	See the following resources in the Lab Toolkit: ▪ *Northwind Traders Technical Specification: Stock Web Site* ▪ *Programming the Login Controls*
	▪ Add a new Web Form to the project and name it **RecoverPassword.aspx**. In the **Add New Item** box, make sure **Select master page** is selected, and then select **sitetemplate.master** as the master page.
	▪ Switch to **Design** view, and then drag a **PasswordRecovery** control onto the Content area.
	▪ On the **Password Recovery Tasks** smart tag, click **AutoFormat** to format the control using the **Elegant** style, and then resize the control to fill the Content area.
	▪ This control adds the ability to e-mail a new password to the e-mail address that was entered during registration.
	By default, ASP.NET stores passwords in a hashed format, so they cannot be recovered. The **PasswordRecovery** control sends a new password to the user that they can use to log on, and then use the Change Password facility (that you will add in the next step) to change to another password of their own choice.
	▪ Edit **Login.aspx**.
	▪ Click the smart tag on the **Login** control and then click **Convert To Template**.
	▪ On the smart tag, click **Edit Templates**.
	▪ Add a new row to the existing table that is used to lay out the controls.

(continued)

Tasks	Supporting information
4. *(continued)*	**Tip** Use the new editing features of Visual Studio 2005 to make this easier:
	■ The Login form is formatted using HTML tables. You need to select a row in the existing table so you can use **the Insert Row Below** option on the **Layout** menu to add a new row easily.
	■ To do this, click anywhere in the row that contains the Password prompt and textbox.
	■ Notice that the bottom of the designer screen shows the nested hierarchy of tags on the page. It begins **<html> <body>** and then shows all the nested tags, ending with the tag of whichever item in the Password row you just clicked.
	■ Starting from the right hand tag in this row, read back to the rightmost **<tr>** tag and click it. By doing this, you select the whole row that contains the Password prompt and textbox.
	■ Click **Insert Row Below** on the **Layout** menu.
	You have inserted a new row below the row containing the Password prompts.
	■ Drag a **Hyperlink** control into the right-hand cell of the new row. Set the text to **"Forgot your password?"** Set the **NavigateUrl** property to **~/RecoverPassword.aspx**.
	■ On the smart tag, click **End Template Editing**.
	Important You can test this part of the application, but you will not be able to send an e-mail, as e-mail has not been set up on the Virtual PC.
5. Give logged-on users the ability to change their password.	See the following resources in the Lab Toolkit:
	■ *Northwind Traders Technical Specification: Stock Web Site*
	■ *Programming the Login Controls*
	■ Add a new Web Form called **profile.aspx** to the project. In the **Add New Item** box, make sure **Select master page** is selected, and then select **sitetemplate.master** as the master page.
	■ Switch to **Design** view, and then drag a **ChangePassword** control onto the Content area.
	■ Use **Auto Format** on the **SmartTags** menu to format the control using the **Elegant** style, and resize it to fill the Content area.
	■ Set the **ContinueDestinationPageURL** property to **~/default.aspx**.
	■ Open siteTemplate.Master for editing.

(continued)

Tasks	Supporting information

5. *(continued)*	▪ Edit the LoggedInTemplate:
	
	  • Drag a **Hyperlink** control from the **Toolbox** and place it to the right of the **LoginStatus** control.
	
	  • Set the **ImageUrl** property of the **Hyperlink** to ~/**Images/profile.gif**.
	
	  • Set the **NavigateUrl** property of the Hyperlink to **Profile.aspx**.

6. Test the application.	▪ The Profile link appears only for logged-on users. ▪ At present, profile.aspx allows users to change only their passwords. However, it would be relatively easy to extend this form to alter other details of the users' profiles.

7. Check the project back into SourceSafe.	▪ Save all changes in Visual Studio 2005.
	
	▪ The configuration changes you made using the ASP.NET Configuration tool created a new ASPNetDB.mdf database in the App_Data folder, but did not add it to the project. Add it now:
	
	  • In Solution Explorer, right-click the **project node**. Click **Add Folder**, and then on the **menu**, click **App_Data** Folder.
	
	  • Right click the **App_Data** folder, and then click **Add Existing Item**. In the **App_Data** folder, click on **ASPNetDB.mdf**, and then click **Add**.
	
	▪ Right-click the project in Solution Explorer and then click **Check in**.
	
	▪ Close Visual Studio 2005.

Exercise 4
Control Access to Content by Using Roles

In this exercise, you will use the ASP.NET Web Site Administration Tool to assign users to roles. You will then implement access control based on the role of the user.

Scenario

It is necessary to further restrict access to certain content on the Northwind Traders Web site. Certain registered users will be members of the Admin role, and only those users are allowed to access the Site Reports page and the Product Reorders page.

Tasks	Supporting information
1. Restart Visual Studio 2005 and run as **Administrator**.	■ From the Windows **Start** Menu, right-click Visual Studio 2005 Beta 2, and then click **Run As**. ■ In the **Run As** dialog, select **The Following User**. Enter **Administrator** for the Username, and **Pa$$w0rd** for the password and then click **OK**. ■ Open the StockMaintenance Web site from Visual SourceSafe in exactly the same way as you did in Exercise 1.
2. Create the Admin role.	See the Lab Toolkit resource *Managing Security with the ASP.NET Web Site Administration Tool*. ■ In this task, you use the ASP.NET Web Site Administration Tool to edit this application's Web.config and ASPNetDB.mdb files. You must check these files out from Visual SourceSafe before running the ASP.NET Web Site Administration Tool. To check out these files, right-click the file in Solution Explorer and then click Check Out for Edit. You can enter a comment in the Check Out For Edit box and then click Check Out. ■ In the ASP.NET Web-Site Administration Tool, create a user called Manager, with a password of Pa$$w0rd. ■ Create the Admin role and put the Manager user in that role.

(*continued*)

Tasks	Supporting information
3. Limit access to ProductReorders.aspx so that only users in the Admin role can access those pages.	▪ Edit the existing event handler for the **Page_Load** event in ProductReorders.aspx in the ProductReorders folder. ▪ Call the **IsInRole** method of the intrinsic **User** object to determine if the current user is in the Admin role. If not, call **Response.Redirect** to redirect to ~/notauthorised.aspx. **Additional Information** You can use the ASP.NET Web Site Administration Tool to manage access to resources by role. This lab demonstrates an alternative technique: to test for role membership in code.
4. Test the application.	▪ Verify that only the Manager can access the **Product Reorders** page. ▪ You have now completed this lab.

Lab Discussion

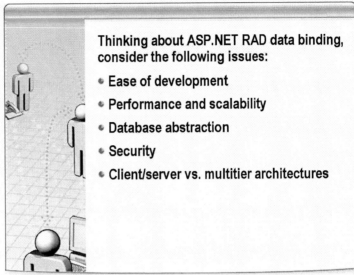

Thinking about ASP.NET RAD data binding, consider the following issues:

- **Ease of development**
- **Performance and scalability**
- **Database abstraction**
- **Security**
- **Client/server vs. multitier architectures**

Now that you have used the RAD data-binding features in Visual Studio 2005, consider their use in developing a business solution. Some issues to consider include:

- Ease of development
- Performance and scalability
- Database abstraction
- Security
- Client/server vs. multitier architectures

You have also learned how to use three enhancements included in ASP.NET 2.0 to develop Web applications using Visual Studio 2005: master pages, site navigation, and themes.

- Discuss with the class the advantages that the enhancements will provide in your workplace.
- Discuss with the class the new or existing applications in your workplace in which you will be able to make best use of the new features.
- Discuss with the class which if any third party or custom solutions can be replaced with these new enhancements to the ASP.NET framework.

Considering the ASP.NET Membership and Role Management features, can you think of any authentication scenarios in which these new facilities are not appropriate?

The default data store for configuration data is an Access database stored in the \data subdirectory of the Web site. In which scenarios is this not appropriate and how would you implement an alternative configuration?

Workshop Evaluation

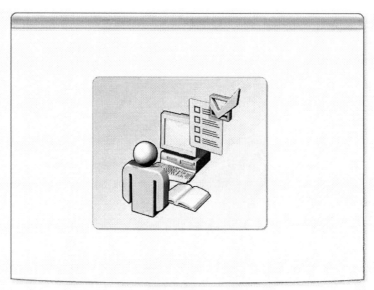

Your evaluation of this workshop will help Microsoft understand the quality of your learning experience.

To complete a workshop evaluation, go to http://www.CourseSurvey.com.

Microsoft will keep your evaluation strictly confidential and will use your responses to improve your future learning experience.

Notes

Notes

Notes

MSM2364BCPWKBK

D0125061836